GOD OF THE
WHIRLWIND

D1475536

GOD OF THE WHIRLWIND

GERALD WHEELER

REVIEW AND HERALD® PUBLISHING ASSOCIATION
HAGERSTOWN, MD 21740

Copyright © 1992
Review and Herald® Publishing Association

The author assumes full responsibility for the accuracy of all
facts and quotations as cited in this book.

This book was
Edited by Raymond H. Woolsey
Designed by Bill Kirstein
Cover art by Superstock; Inset: J. E. Seward
Type set: 11.5/12.5 Zapf Book Light

PRINTED IN U.S.A.

97 96 95 94 93 92   10 9 8 7 6 5 4 3 2 1

Unless otherwise noted, Bible texts in this book are from the New Revised
Standard Version of the Bible, copyright © 1989 by the Division of Christian
Education of the National Council of the Churches of Christ in the U.S.A. Used
by permission.

Bible texts credited to Jerusalem are from *The Jerusalem Bible*, copyright ©
1966 by Darton, Longman & Todd, Ltd., and Doubleday & Company, Inc. Used
by permission of the publisher.

Bible texts credited to Moffatt are from: *The Bible: A New Translation*, by James
Moffatt. Copyright by James Moffatt 1954. Used by permission of Harper &
Row, Publishers, Incorporated.

Bible texts credited to RSV are from the Revised Standard Version of the Bible,
copyright © 1946, 1952, 1971, by the Division of Christian Education of the National Council of the Churches of Christ in the U.S.A. Used by permission.

Library of Congress Cataloging in Publication Data
Wheeler, Gerald.
    God of the whirlwind / Gerald Wheeler.
        p.   cm.
    Includes bibliographical references.
    1. Bible. O.T. Job—Criticism, interpretation, etc.   I. Title.
BS1415.2.W474   1992
223'.106—dc20   92-33030
                                                                CIP

ISBN 0-8280-0694-6

Dedication

To Tompaul
Who wants to know

Contents

A Story for All Time

A FRIEND recently told me of a religious convocation she attended several years ago. Before the main meeting began, one of the men on the platform began interviewing selected people from the audience. The first person stood and haltingly told a heart-gripping story of the loss of a young child to leukemia. His wife could barely control her emotions. The scene left my friend in tears.

The next person interviewed had a similar story, a child with leukemia. But in this case the disease had gone into remission, and the parents believed that God had divinely healed him. The leader on the platform, forgetting the previous couple's experience, began to exclaim how the Lord had truly blessed the family. The parents joyously echoed him, repeating over and over how good the Lord had been to them.

My friend kept thinking to herself, *I wonder how the first couple are reacting to this? Are they asking themselves, "What about us? Why didn't God heal our child? Why did He let our child die and heal this couple's? Were they better people than we were?"*

The problem of suffering is one of the most difficult questions we face in our lives. We encounter suffering in some form everywhere. It strikes everyone. A respected religious leader about to participate in the joy of a wedding gets rushed to a hospital emergency room instead, where the physicians diagnose him as having a brain tumor. An automobile accident snuffs out the life of a bright and talented young person about to embark on a promising career. For a few moments a busy parent loses track of a child, then discovers that he has wandered off and drowned in a shallow pond. A trusted business partner, who is also a fellow church member, embezzles and destroys a company built up over many years of sacrifice. Disease cripples the bodies of loved ones. Malicious gossip shatters the reputations, careers, and lives of friends and associates. Each of us could cite dozens of heart-wrenching examples. Life seems one unending series of numbing tragedies.

And always the question rages through our minds, *Why?* Our friends and loved ones didn't deserve to have that happen to them. They were never that bad. Where is justice in life? Where is God when tragedies take place? Why does He let them happen? Doesn't He have the power to stop them? If He does, why does He just sit there as His creation writhes in agony? Does He get some kind of perverse joy out of watching suffering? Is He punishing people far out of proportion to the deed? Questions—unending questions—they can haunt us day and night.

Such questions are not new. We know that humanity has struggled with similar ones as long as it has kept written records. Six fragments of a clay tablet from the Sumerian city of Nippur (c. 2000 B.C.) record its unknown author's protest against undeserved suffering. The document, commonly called by scholars "A Man and His God," offers as its answer, "Never has a sinless child been born to its mother." It concludes that we all suffer because we are all sinful. But that doesn't explain what we instinctively know are cases of disproportionate suffering.

A 1400-1200 B.C. document entitled "Ludlul Bel Nemeqi [I Will Praise the Lord of Wisdom]" tells how a man named Subsi-mesre-Sakkan endured various disasters before the Mesopotamian god Marduk restored him to his former state. Called by many "The Babylonian Job," it asks, "Why does Marduk allow his servant to suffer?" and concludes that no matter how unjustified such suffering might appear to be, the victim should keep on glorifying his god until the deity decides to respond to his prayers. The gods are inscrutable and their actions are simply beyond human understanding. But who can worship—let alone love—a god who seems indifferent or distant?

Another set of tablets from the ancient library of Ashurbanipal preserves an acrostic dialogue between a sufferer and his friend. The friend defends his culture's understanding of how the universe and society is supposed to operate against the complaints of the suffering individual. Scholars often refer to it as the "Babylonian Theodicy." (A theodicy attempts to defend God's goodness despite the existence of evil.[1])

Two Egyptian works, the "Protests of the Eloquent Peasant" and the "Admonitions of Ipu-Wer," also deal with the issue of undeserved suffering. Some have considered an Akkadian fable known as the "Dispute Between the Date Palm and Tamarisk" as similar to these other works. Writings on the question of suffering, often using the dialogue form, also appeared in Greek literature and elsewhere.[2]

But apparently none of these have diminished the impact of the most famous of all ancient theodicies, or defenses of God, against the question of suffering, the Old Testament book of Job. In the words of Edwin M. Good, "Job seems unique in the ancient world, with no clear indication that its dialogue was influenced in style or form by these other works." [3]

And, unlike the previous ancient documents that are known to only a few scholars, the book of Job has captured humanity's imagination for centuries. It has even intrigued modern secular writers who have used its themes and approach as a powerful vehicle to comment on human problems. The poets Archibald MacLeish ("J.B.") and Robert Frost ("A Mask of Reason") found inspiration in it. Novelist Joseph Roth (*Job*) and the science fiction writer Robert Heinlein (*Job—A Comedy of Justice*) wrote novels patterned after the book, and playwright Neil Simon produced a play titled *God's Favorite*.

Even modern composers such as Luigi Dallapiccola and Ralph Vaughan Williams have produced music with Job in mind. The power of a great work like Job is that each generation can keep coming back to it and find it speaking to new situations and problems.

"Focusing as it does on issues of suffering and the questions it raises," J. Gerald Janzen observes, "the book of Job has a universal appeal, in some respects unique in the Scriptures of the Judaeo-Christian tradition." [4]

One of the reasons that it still has the power to speak to those struggling with the dilemma of undeserved suffering is that it offers no simple answers, as did the ancient theodicies. Most people who know something about the book assume that it resolves the eternal question by revealing that Satan is responsible for all suffering. The prologue and epilogue stick in their memory, and they assume that is all there is to the book.

But, as we shall see, Job is not that simple. On the contrary, its extreme complexity has left scholars, theologians, commentators, and just plain believers debating its fundamental message and meaning for centuries.

The book raises uncomfortable questions and issues that can trouble even the most devout reader. In fact, these questions can be so disturbing to religious sensibilities that when the Jews translated the Old Testament into Greek, a version known as the Septuagint, they deliberately toned down many such passages. Edwin Good observes that "modern scholarship has shown how thoroughly this version [The Septuagint] eviscerated the hard edge of the Joban arguments." [5] The author of Job knew that hard questions must often be wrestled with.

The book of Job is not a calm, dispassionate presentation of inside information about suffering or the conflict between good and evil. Rather, it presents an intense, traumatic, and emotional struggle by a handful of human beings trying to find meaning and faith in God and His ways. And we, as modern readers, must learn how to interpret what they said to make it relevant for our own times.

The controversy surrounding the book involves not only its message, but also the issue of who wrote it, when, and how. Tradition says that Moses authored it, but its language, literary style, and themes are so elusive that scholars have tried to peg it into many different centuries and have offered countless reconstructions of its literary history. For many decades biblical scholars argued that it was late in origin, perhaps from the time of the exile or even afterward. More recently a growing number of scholars have pushed the book back further in time, as further research has raised doubts about the kinds of arguments used to support a late date.[6] Roland E. Murphy, a noted scholar on the book of Job, once commented that while its language has many old elements, the evidence is so ambiguous that one could almost take one's choice of a date.

Although the poetic parts of Job have words of Aramaic, Arabic, Akkadian, and Egyptian origin, the narrative is written in a highly literary "classical" Hebrew, with no evidence of any regional dialect that might suggest where it was written. The book as a whole contains many words and grammatical forms that appear nowhere else in the Hebrew Scriptures, and it has sections that make little or no known grammatical sense in its present form. Translations of such passages can be little more than educated guesses based on tradition or a juggling of the text. Recent translations have reminded readers of this fact through special footnotes. The New Revised Standard Version, for example, employs the phrase "meaning of Heb. uncertain." If the abbreviation "Cn" (correction) appears, it indicates that the committee that oversaw the translation agreed with competent scholars "as to the most probable reconstruction of the original text." The New International Version and the *Revised English*

Bible have similar footnotes to remind the reader of the difficulty of the original Hebrew. Only the book of Hosea presents more problems in translation.

The prose style of chapters 1, 2, and 42 is relatively simple, while the rest of the book, except for one-line introductions to the speeches and Job 32:1-5, consists of complex and often sublime poetry. Each line of poetry, coinciding with the numbered verses that appear in modern Bibles, has two halves. Each of the halves will say almost exactly the same thing, though they also may either complement or contrast with each other. When the author wanted to emphasize something, the line would have three parts instead of two. [7]

Most readers remember the prose part and skim over the far larger poetic section, thus missing major themes of the book. Scholars have long argued that the prose part came first and that later authors or editors added the poetic passages. There may well have been an earlier core, [8] but any reconstruction of the book's literary history is only speculation. As Good reminds us: "All such conclusions can be no more than guesses, as we have no copies of Job representing these stages." [9]

This present book will concentrate solely on the text of Job as we have it now, what scholars call the canonical Job.

The Hebrew Scriptures always linked Job with the books of Psalms and Proverbs, Psalms coming first in order and Job and Proverbs then alternating in sequence. Scholars have sometimes taken where the Hebrew Bible put a particular book in its major divisions as a clue to its dating, but the evidence here is at best ambiguous. The Septuagint put Job in various arrangements, one manuscript even having it at the end of the Old Testament, after the apocryphal book of Ecclesiasticus. The Syriac Bible placed it between the Pentateuch and Joshua, probably because of the tradition of Moses as author.

Scholars often consider the book as an example of wisdom literature, a widespread literary form in the ancient world. The Egyptians and Mesopotamians, in addition to the Israelites, wrote on how to deal with the practical issues of everyday life, as well as how to understand and cope with troubling moral problems. Most wisdom writers believed that one could find ultimate wisdom only in the gods.

Generally, wisdom authors composed proverbs and aphorisms. In them they discussed moral and behavioral topics, and how to achieve success in life (for example, the righteous person is wise and successful in all that he does, while the fool is wicked and doomed to failure). Also, they sought inspiration and guidance in the world of nature. The biblical books generally considered to belong to the wisdom category include Proverbs, Ecclesiastes, and certain psalms, as well as Job. [10]

But though Job is interested in wisdom and nature, it has some major differences. Unlike the other biblical wisdom books, Job employs a dialogue structure and partial narration. While Job's friends quote many of the positions and arguments that the wise espouse in Proverbs and elsewhere, the book of Job condemns the friends as wrong in their understanding. One commentator has suggested that Job belongs to the wisdom category "as the exception to its rigidities." [11]

The book of Job consists of five basic parts:

1. Prologue (in prose), where Job suffers tragedy (1:1-2:13)

2. Job dialogues with his three friends (3:1-31:40)

3. Speeches of Elihu (32:1-37:24)

4. Dialogue with God (38:1-42:6)

5. Epilogue (in prose), where God restores Job (42:7-17).

As is characteristic of the rest of the Hebrew Scriptures, the book of Job prefers conversation to third-person narration or description. Biblical conversation presents the kind of information that a modern writer would put into description or regular narration. The Old Testament follows a rule that only two people can speak to each other at a time, and in the case of Job, [12] people speak essentially in monologues. Only in the prologue and epilogue, and possibly chapter 28, do we hear the direct voice of the author.

Old Testament writers seldom make their own comments on the events they are portraying. The modern reader must thus be extra alert to catch their viewpoint, either through the words of the biblical character or in some more indirect way. [13]

W. F. Albright has interpreted Job's name as meaning "Where is (my) Father?" Other suggestions have included "be an enemy," either in the sense of being an opponent of God or His victim, and, basing it on an Arab root, "one who repents." [14]

The name appears in second millennium B.C. Akkadian documents from Mari and Alalakh, the Amarna letters (clay tablets written from Palestine to the Egyptian pharaohs about 1350 B.C.), and Egyptian Execration texts of about 2000 B.C. (The Egyptians would write the names of their enemies on pieces of pottery and break them so as to put a curse on their foes.) The Jobs mentioned in these texts were tribal leaders in the Palestinian region. [15]

Job is not an Israelite, as Jewish tradition has long recognized and emphasized. [16] Rather, he is one of a number of non-Israelite individuals that the Old Testament portrays as worshipers of the true God. Melchizedek, king of Salem (the future site of Jerusalem; it remained a pagan enclave among the Israelites until David captured it), blessed Abraham and accepted tithe and offerings after the patriarch returned in triumph from battle. Balaam, a non-Israelite prophet, had a relationship with the true God, as did Jethro, Moses' father-in-law and a priest among the Midianites. (The rest of the Midianites were idolaters who joined the Moabites in seducing Israel into idolatry as God's people prepared to enter the Promised Land. See Num. 25.)

Several scholars have suggested that the Old Testament also seems to imply that at least some of the people of Shechem might have worshiped the true God in some way. They point out that the patriarchs often visited there. Scripture does not mention the city as being destroyed during the Israelite invasion of Canaan, and the Israelites held a large rally on the nearby slopes of Mount Ebal and Mount Gerizim (Joshua 8:30-35). Later, Shechem became a residence city of the Kohathite Levites (Joshua 21:20, 21).

Although the Old Testament focuses on the chosen line, it does hint that God is always reaching out to the people of the other nations. In time, God's people could even conceive of such nations as Egypt and Assyria worshiping the God of Israel and being equals

18

with Israel (Isa. 19:19-24). [17] The God of Israel was the God of all men and women. He would reach out to all who would respond to Him. [18]

The fact that Job was not an Israelite may have also appealed to Israelite readers because it demonstrated the universality of suffering. Suffering extends beyond every ethnic and geographical boundary and has troubled every person that has ever lived. It is not a possession unique to God's people. In addition, Job as a non-Israelite could be quoted as saying things in his agony and frustration that might have made pious readers uncomfortable if they had come from the lips of an Israelite. Even then, as pointed out earlier, the translators of the Septuagint felt a need to tone down, or soften, many of his statements.

Scholars generally agree that several of the book's characters come from places in Edom, southeast of Israel and in what is now modern Jordan. We see a world where desert and cultivated land exist close together. Teman (Job 2:11), for example, is generally associated throughout the Old Testament with Edom (Jer. 49:7, 20; Eze. 25:13; Amos 1:11; Obadiah 8, 9), though some have connected it with the Tema in Arabia. Genesis links the name Eliphaz with Edom (Gen. 36:11, 15).

At first glance the reader might assume that Job was merely a desert dweller like the modern Bedouin of the region, but in chapter 29 and elsewhere we find many allusions to an urban world. Most likely the patriarch was a seminomad who lived in a walled city part of the year and migrated with his flocks the rest of the time.

Yet, except for those limited hints, the book is extremely vague in its setting, especially the historical situation it took place in. J. Gerald Janzen has even suggested that it "is as though a deliberate effort had been made to pose the problems raised in the book in general human terms, by removing the story from a specifically Israelite setting." [19] All of us face suffering, even in our modern technological world, and all of us need the same hope and assurance that the ancient patriarch sought; a book with a more universal approach speaks more clearly to us.

Job is a deep and often disturbing book. As we study it we may find ourselves uncomfortable. Suffering itself is a frightening matter. Nor does the book provide simple answers. It only points in directions where we might find such answers.

In Job we will encounter issues that traditional piety might prefer to gloss over or even reject. But unless we face them, we will miss the full and honest message of this divinely inspired book. It is a message that will raise even more questions than it answers. But it is a message every one of us needs, to survive in the storms of our complex and terrifying world. [20]

---

[1] Translations of these ancient documents appear in James Pritchard, ed., *Ancient Near Eastern Texts*, 3rd ed. (Princeton, N.J.: Princeton University Press, 1969). John H. Walton discusses their relationship to the biblical book of Job in his *Israelite Literature in Its Cultural Context* (Grand Rapids: Zondervan, 1989), pp. 169-187.

[2] Victor H. Matthews and Don C. Benjamin have produced a new translation of these texts that is more concerned with the sense and less with technical grammatical details. They also group the texts according to their resemblance to Old Testament passages. See their *Old Testament Parallels: Laws and Stories From the Ancient Near East* (New York: Paulist Press, 1991), pp. 201-224.

[3] Edwin M. Good, "Job," in *Harper's Bible Commentary*, ed. James L. Mays (San Francisco: Harper and Row, 1988), p. 409.

[4] J. Gerald Janzen, *Job* (Interpretation: A Commentary for Teaching and Preaching) (Atlanta: John Knox Press, 1985), p. 1.

[5] Good, p. 409.

[6] The book is full of details of the patriarchal age. It describes Job's wealth in terms of flocks and servants. He offers sacrifice at a local shrine. The Sabeans and the Chaldeans are

marauding tribes rather than settled city dwellers.

Fragments of a manuscript of Job found at Qumran are written in paleo-Hebrew letters, suggesting that the book had a long tradition of being considered as coming from the patriarchal age.

Those who argue that Job was written during the Exilic period have to deal with the fact that it contains no specific references or allusions to the exile.

[7] A. van Selms, *Job: A Practical Commentary* (Grand Rapids: Eerdmans, 1985), p. 5.

[8] David Penchansky, in *The Betrayal of God: Ideological Conflict in Job* (Louisville: Westminster/John Knox Press, 1990), page 38, points out that the prologue "does not unequivocally support the law of retribution. Job's willingness to receive 'evil from Yahweh' as well as the good, questions some of the chief views of Israelite theology on the predictability of God." Elsewhere in his book Penchansky speculates that later authors or editors may have developed themes and questions that were latent in the prose framework or basic story to meet new problems that had arisen. Expansion or revision of a biblical document can be accommodated even within a conservative concept of inspiration. For example, the Septuagint and other ancient manuscripts of the book of Jeremiah varied by 40 percent and had greatly different arrangements of the material within the book, indicating that God's people were willing to accept some modifications of an inspired book. Interestingly, in the Septuagint, the Greek translation of the Old Testament, the book of Job is 360-400 lines shorter than the Hebrew text. The translation omitted many repetitious passages.

[9] Good, p. 408.

[10] Roland E. Murphy, one of the leading scholars of wisdom literature, offers a convenient summary of the characteristics of the wisdom tradition in his *Wisdom Literature and Psalms* (Nashville: Abingdon Press, 1983).

[11] Good, p. 409.

[12] Robert Alter, *The Art of Biblical Narrative* (New York: Basic Books, 1981), pp. 63-87.

[13] *Ibid.*, p. 37, *passim.*

[14] William Sanford La Sor, David Allan Hubbard, and Frederic William Bush, *Old Testament Survey: The Message, Form, and Background of the Old Testament* (Grand Rapids: Eerdmans, 1982), p. 560.

[15] Marvin H. Pope, *Job*, 3rd ed. (Garden City, N.Y.: Doubleday, 1979), pp. 5f; W. F. Albright, "Northwest-Semitic Names in a List of Egyptian Slaves From the Eighteenth Century B.C." *Journal of the American Oriental Society* 74 (1954), pp. 222-233.

[16] The Septuagint, however, has Job as a grandson of Esau and the fifth generation from Abraham, tying him closer to Israel.

[17] For a discussion of the relationship with the other nations that the prophets held out to God's people, see Donald E. Gowan, *Eschatology in the Old Testament* (Philadelphia: Fortress Press, 1986), pp. 48-54.

[18] The poetic speeches use pre-Mosaic names for God—names shared by the surrounding people in Palestine—while the prose prologue and epilogue remind the reader that behind these older names is Yahweh of Israel, the one and only true God of the universe (Norman C. Habel, *The Book of Job* [Philadelphia: Westminster Press, 1985], pp. 39, 40).

[19] J. Gerald Janzen, *Job* (Atlanta: John Knox Press, 1985), p. 5.

[20] Limits of space do not permit a verse-by-verse commentary. Instead, this book will explore only certain themes of this complex and fascinating biblical book.

God's Servant

2

"THERE was once a man in the land of Uz whose name was Job. That man was blameless and upright, one who feared God and turned away from evil" (Job 1:1).

The book of Job begins with a dreamy, distant quality that scholars are fond of comparing to a folk story. The terse prose portions give only a bare minimum of detail, a style that reminds one of stories in Genesis, Judges, and Ruth.[1] Old Testament narrative was extremely sparse in setting and description. It made every word count and depended on nuances rather than extensive detail, requiring the reader to pay close attention not only to what the writer said but often to what he didn't.

Job lives in the unknown land of Uz, somewhere in the "east" (verse 3). To the ancient Israelite, "east" was anything on the other side of the Jordan River, a vague territory extending from Midian in the south to Aram-naharaim in the north.[2] It included both desert and fertile agricultural land that could periodically support a respectable urban population.

Here, in one of the few places in the book where the author speaks directly to the reader, he describes Job not only as a worshiper of the true God, the God of Israel, but as "blameless and upright," or more literally, "complete and straight." The patriarch's virtuous character compels him to turn away from all evil. [3] David Noel Freedman believes that there cannot be a valid interpretation of the book of Job that does not begin with this premise. [4]

Next, the author records that Job had a large family of seven sons and three daughters (both numbers and their sum being considered symbols of completeness). He had large herds of livestock (the major form of wealth in the ancient world) and ample servants to care for them. Thus Job "was the greatest of all the people of the east" (verse 3). The reader instantly assumes that God has blessed him for his exemplary life. Because he has been a good man, he has wealth, a large family, and the other good things valued by the biblical world. Only gentle zephyrs stir the tranquillity of his life.

John C. L. Gibson observes that such a description will jar the modern reader because it appears to imply that Job received his prosperity as a reward for his virtue. He reminds us that Christians usually phrase things more cautiously because "we do not readily ascribe sainthood to anybody, and, when we do, we demand that our saints have as few of this world's goods as possible. We are too ingrained with Paul's teaching—that human beings cannot earn God's approval by their own good works—to be impressed by a character reference like the one here given to Job." [5]

As Christian readers we must remember that the book of Job is not dealing with Job's character from the viewpoint of salvation, but simply that he was—when seen from a human perspective—a good man who lived his religion and had a definite and trusting relationship with his God. He was not good in the theological sense that his virtuous character saved him. Rather, the narrator wants us to see that God accepted and respected Job's moral qualities as he lived them day to day.

Job had flaws, as he himself acknowledged (i.e., Job 13:26 and 14:16, 17), but he still exemplified how a pious man should treat his fellow human beings and worship his God. The patriarch was God's servant on earth. Thus the issue of the book is not whether Job is worthy of being saved, but whether he deserved the tragedies that devastated his life.

Job's sons enjoyed their father's wealth by holding feasts in turn in each other's houses. Commentators have variously interpreted the feasts as weekly events, cultic feast days, or even birthdays. In a culture in which women did not eat with men and kept out of sight, the sisters received the unusual honor of being invited to eat and drink with their male siblings. (The daughters Job had after his restoration, according to Job 42:15, also received unusual honor.)

After each feast Job would present burnt offerings lest "my children have sinned, and cursed God in their hearts" (Job 1:5). The word translated "curse" usually means "bless" but has been translated "curse" also in Job 2:5, 9; 1 Kings 21:10, 13; and Psalm 10:3 because the context makes no sense with the literal meaning. Simundson suggests that the word acquired the additional and exact opposite meaning because of "religious sensitivities about the name of God." [6] It illustrates the kind of difficulties translators face when they attempt to render an ancient language into a modern one.

Commentators have puzzled over Job's behavior, some even suggesting that he didn't quite trust his family's spiritual life, while others have seen in the practice a positive and admirable concern for their spiritual welfare.

Suddenly the scene shifts from Job's idyllic life on earth to the mysterious courts of heaven. The book looks at what will happen to Job from two sharply contrasting perspectives. The issues that the patriarch and his friends will see in his experience are quite different from those that will concern the heavenly watchers.

The narrator depicts the heavenly beings presenting themselves before Yahweh, the God of Israel and the ruler of the universe. Scripture occasionally mentions God meeting with the heavenly assembly (1 Kings 22:19; Isa. 6:1; Ps. 82:1; 89:5, 7). The pagan mythologies of Canaan and Mesopotamia also described heavenly assemblies where the lesser gods met with the ruling deity.

Mingling with the heavenly hosts is Satan, or in the Hebrew, *HaSatan* with the definite article. The term *the Satan* appears several times in the Old Testament and indicates a legal opponent or prosecutor. For example, in Zechariah 3 the Satan acts as the prosecuting attorney to bring a charge of cultic defilement against Joshua, the high priest of the Temple. The verb form of *satan* means "to oppose." Modern versions of the Bible will footnote the name with such translations as "accuser" or "the adversary."

Scholars repeatedly remind us that the Old Testament does not develop the character of Satan as fully as does the New Testament. They may either reject any connection between the Satan here and that of the New Testament, [7] or reduce him to little more than a roving ambassador or spy who reports anything wrong to God and even upholds His honor. [8]

The Old Testament concentrates on Satan's activity of bringing accusations or charges against God's people. Why the Hebrew Scriptures do not portray him in the detail that the New Testament does, we can only speculate. Perhaps part of the reason was the Old Testament's emphasis on maintaining the sovereignty of Yahweh as the only true God.

To preserve the concept of monotheism, its writers increasingly denied the possibility of any rival to God. The ancient world had many pairs of gods struggling with each other, such as Set and Osiris in Egyptian mythology. In Mesopotamia Marduk struggled with Tiamat, and Baal of Canaan had his rivals.

Perhaps because God was seeking to get across to His people that He was the only and all-powerful God, He did not want to confuse them by prematurely introducing the concept of some being who was struggling with Him for control of the world. In Exodus 4:11 and elsewhere He was even willing to accept responsibility for blindness, deafness, and other tragedies. To have stressed Satan's power and cunning would have reminded a people still steeped in polytheism too much of the pagan concepts around them.

But, as La Sor, Hubbard, and Bush remind us, the portrayal of Satan in the book of Job will anticipate his role elsewhere in Scripture. "He is a creature of God, yet an enemy of God's will (cf. Matt. 4:1-11; Luke 4:1-13). He seeks to plague God's people both physically (2 Cor. 12:7) and spiritually (2 Cor. 11:14). He has been defeated by Christ's obedience and will disappear from the story at the end (Rev. 20:2, 7, 10)." [9]

Andersen comments that while Satan's insolence reveals a mind already hostile to God, the book does not depict him as a rival on a par with the Deity. It presents no form of dualism. "The Satan may be the chief mischief-maker of the universe, but he is a mere creature, puny compared with the Lord. He can do only what God permits him to do." [10] And the reader must never forget that fact.

The Satan has made his appearance, and the drama now begins. God asks him where he has come from (Job 1:6, 7), and the Satan replies that he has been inspecting the earth (verse 7). It appears to be a hostile examination, as if he is looking for something to criticize or use against God. The Lord then asks him if he has "considered my servant Job?" (verse 8).

The question is clearly a leading one. Contrary to what some scholars charge, God is doing more here than merely bragging. If the Satan has been roving the earth as he said, then he has to know about Job—as becomes obvious in his response to God's question. The Lord also raises the question in the presence of the assembly of heavenly beings. They are watching and listening, and He has more in mind than showing off a loyal human being. The forthcoming demonstration of Job's character is for them more than for Satan. The accuser has already made up his mind about the human being. He thinks that he understands what drives Job, but he is wrong. Only God can see into the man's motivations, into his innermost character. But at least God tries to help him see what makes the patriarch tick.

J. Gerald Janzen suggests that God's question not only seeks to direct the Satan's attention to Job, but to raise a specific question in that being's mind. [11] It is a question He wants the rest of heaven's assembly to catch also. God further shapes that question by echoing the narrator's description of Job in verse 1 and adding that there was no one else on earth like the patriarch.

The Satan responds as God intended, and demands, "Does Job fear God for nothing?" (verse 9). [12] Here is perhaps the most fundamental question that the book wrestles with. Yes, we all want to know why suffering comes, but even more important is Why are the righteous pious? How will a person respond when suffering strikes and that person doesn't deserve it?

God clearly has blessed Job. Is that why he worships Him? Will he remain loyal if that motivation of divine blessing should vanish? Will he continue to believe that God is inherently worthy of being worshiped? Why do created beings worship God? It is an ancient question that Satan first raised in the Garden of Eden, [13] and he is still pressing it here. The book will not answer it directly. It will let us see only how Job responds to suffering that he believes has come from God Himself.

The Satan charges that God has protected and prospered Job, and that the man naturally has every reason to cling to Him. Janzen says that the Satan is in a way partially right, because Job has a reason for "fearing" or worshiping, God—"he fears God in grateful response for his creatural existence." [14] "But stretch out your hand now, and touch all that he has, and he will curse you to your face" (verse 11), the Satan taunts.

David Noel Freedman suggests the Satan is insinuating that Job has been hoodwinking God by only pretending to be righteous. Should God strip away Job's material possessions and blessings, the Deity would soon discover both that the patriarch had been using Him and that the man's piety and righteousness was shallow and superficial. [15]

Edwin M. Good views the Satan's statement in verse 11 as a self-curse. [16] In verse 12 God allows the Satan to find out if Job will respond as he claims, but nothing must happen to the man himself. Here and in the next chapter, God permits the Satan to go only to a certain point in his attack on Job and no further.

Notice that the Satan puts the responsibility for what he plans to do on God, even though, as verse 12 clearly indicates, he will be the direct cause of the disasters. Also, God only delegates to the Satan the power to afflict Job. As we have observed before, the Old Testament reserves all power to God, even that of evil.

God takes a great risk when He trusts Job to the Satan's challenge. True, He does know Job in the deepest part of his soul, but the man still has the freedom to turn against Him if he so chooses. Yet God is willing to accept the risk in front of the divine assembly because He has confidence in a person He has known from intimate relationship. Crenshaw and Freedman compare Job's experience to that of Abraham. [17]

Job is not the only one on trial here, and the heavenly assembly knows it. The patriarch is God's servant, but what is the Master like? Is He a cosmic despot that has to bribe the loyalty of His subjects? Can

He really inspire devotion even if His blessings are withheld? Is He really worthy of being God? Job's response will show.

The disasters now begin. A raiding party of Sabeans, nomads from Arabia, attack and kill his farmhands, carrying off the animals (verses 13-15). The text mentions that the raid occurred on one of the family feast days, perhaps the day of the feast cycle that Job offered sacrifices for his children's protection.[18] Only one servant survives to report the calamity.

"The fire of God" (verse 16) wipes out Job's flocks of sheep and slays all but one of his herdsmen. Next, Chaldean raiders capture his camel herds and slaughter all but one of the men guarding them (verse 17). Finally, the worst disaster of all happens. A great wind, whipping suffocating clouds of dust in from the desert, strikes the oldest son's house and crushes Job's children (verses 18, 19).[19] Again the Satan makes sure that someone will survive to bring the news to Job. That whirlwind from the desert will blast more than just a house—it will lash its fury against religious faith.

Job's sacrifices for his children have been of no avail. The Lord has not protected them.[20] In fact, fire and wind are God's personal weapons. Does Job see divine fingerprints in these disasters? Numbly he goes through the ancient Near Eastern ritual of grief, tearing his clothes and shaving his head. But he still clings to his God. Throwing himself to the ground, he prays, perhaps in a state of profound shock, "Naked I came from my mother's womb, and naked shall I return there; the Lord gave, and the Lord has taken away blessed be the name of the Lord" (verse 21).[21]

How much he has actually thought through what

he says we have no way of knowing. Probably his overwhelming shock and numb grief blind him to many of the implications of his words. But those who argue that the prologue and epilogue depict a different God than that of the poetic part of the book overlook verse 21. God can bring both good *and* bad. Job may still worship his God, but what questions lurk just below his consciousness?

The voice of the narrator, speaking directly to the reader perhaps to emphasize the point, declares that Job did not sin, nor has he yet accused God of wrongdoing (verse 22).

The scene returns to heaven. In a pattern common in Hebrew narrative,[22] Job 2:1-3 repeats the question and answer of Job 1:6-8. God does add, though, "he still persists in his integrity, although you incited me against him, to destroy him for no reason" (verse 3). Notice that God here accepts at least partial responsibility for what has happened to Job. And all the while He and the Satan are speaking, the assembled sons of God are watching and listening with rapt attention.

Perhaps an incident from World War II will give us an insight into God's predicament. The Germans had developed a sophisticated code machine called Enigma to transmit military messages that they then shared with their Axis partners. Through a fortunate series of events the British obtained a copy of the code machine and set up a special intelligence group to decode Axis military radio transmissions. But the British had to protect the secret of their advantage at all costs. Whenever the Allies attacked Axis targets or intercepted a German or Japanese military strike, they had to make it appear that they had come across the information by accident. If they bombed a ship convoy, they would send a spotter plane over it first and allow it to be seen by the enemy before sending in the attack planes. Even so, they nearly blew their cover when they shot down a Japanese aircraft carrying the most important Japanese admiral without first going through the ruse of "accidentally" spotting the plane.

Ordinarily the Germans identified their targets by number. Once, though, they slipped and named a forthcoming air raid objective as Coventry, England. Winston Churchill had to decide whether to alert the city of the impending raid—and risk exposing the Allies' ability to decode German military messages—or let the city be destroyed and protect the secret that had so far tipped the balance of military power in favor of the Allied Forces. The British prime minister chose the latter.

God had to risk Job to answer the questions the Satan was raising in the minds of the watching heavenly assembly.

According to God's response to the Satan, Job is still blameless and upright. The divine testimonial challenges our pat answers of what God expects of us. From chapter 3 onward he will not live up to common Christian stereotypes of how a believer and worshiper should behave.

No matter how we might view God's foreknowledge, the anger and hurt and frustration that soon surface had to be already there in Job's basic character. Yet the Lord could still call Job in the presence not only of the Satan but also the rest of the divine host, "a blameless and upright man who fears God and turns away from evil" (verse 3). Perhaps God's definition of blameless and upright is broader and shows more understanding than many human ones.

Exploding in frustration and defeat, the Satan snaps, "Skin for skin! All that people have they will give to save their lives" (verse 4). We no longer know all that the apparently proverbial phrase "skin for skin" implied. Gibson suggests that it might have the meaning of "[A man, if he has to, will surrender someone else's] skin [life] for [to save] [his own] skin [life]." [23] Others see the skin as referring to animal hides, thus making the phrase a proverb used by tradesmen. But whatever it meant, clearly the Satan attacked Job's character, and by implication the God he worshiped and had a deep relationship with.

Again the Lord takes a great risk—and at the same time gives Job an even greater honor, that of defending God Himself. It is doubtful that Job would have appreciated that honor, however.

Many readers of the book of Job find themselves greatly disturbed by the seemingly callous way that God "used" Job to prove a point. But God realized that the stakes were high. The heavenly assembly had been watching, and God knew what they were thinking. *Was Satan right? What really did motivate Job? And if Job was as the Satan claimed, what, then, about the God the man worshiped?* As Freedman puts it, the assembled sons of God are "not merely echoes or sycophants of the Almighty, they are intelligent, serious and significant actors" who have a role in heavenly decision-making. [24]

Although the poetic dialogues beginning in chapter 3 might make it appear that only Job is on trial before his friends, the reader knows that Someone else also stands in the dock. As Peter C. Craigie asks, What kind of God will permit the innocent to go through what Job does? "The atheist and the theist in this world may both suffer terribly, without any evident reason for their agony, but the theist—whose God is supposed to be just and merciful—may suffer the more profound spiritual agony. Is it really possible to believe in a God of justice in a world marked by such apparently unjust suffering?" [25] While what happens to Job does not answer such questions directly, it does have a tremendous bearing on them.

The Satan suggested that while a man might accept the loss of everything he has, it was quite another matter to have his body attacked (Job 2:5). Contrary to those who believe in a dualism of body and soul, we are our bodies, and when something happens to them, it affects us in the deepest and most profound sense.

Modern scientific research is continually demonstrating the intimate and unbreakable connection between the brain—the seat of our consciousness—and the rest of the body. What affects the body impacts on the brain—and thus the mind and its spiritual thoughts; and what occurs in the mind will influence the body. Try to pray when your tooth aches, your stomach is upset, or your body is exhausted from heavy work, lack of sleep, or emotional stress. On the other hand, notice how your spiritual thoughts soar after a brisk walk on a cool sunny day.

Satan had gone after Job's world—now he was attacking the innermost Job himself. In the words of Daniel J. Simundson, "It is one thing to suffer the loss of wealth or even the death of loved ones, but the real crunch comes when one's own self is under attack." [26]

A second time the Satan seeks to put the blame of the forthcoming suffering on God Himself—"Stretch out your hand now and touch his bone and his flesh, and he will curse you to your face" (verse 5). And a second time God reminds the Satan and the watching heavenly assembly that he, Satan, is the direct cause of Job's trials—"he is in your power"—but that he can go so far and no further against God's servant (verse 6).

Job now reels from Satan's final attack. God had demanded that the Satan spare the man's life, but the patriarch will find no comfort in that protection. The pain of the "loathsome sores" (verse 7) covering his whole body is excruciating.

Though the book will later list a number of his symptoms, they are not precise enough to diagnose his condition. Contrary to at least one tradition, it is probably not the modern form of leprosy, but one of the other skin diseases rampant in the Near East.[27] The only relief he can find from the almost overwhelming pain is to scrape himself with one of the potsherds that littered the surface of the ground around every Near Eastern village and town. He sits in the ashes, an ancient symbol of mourning and grief.

But Job suffers from more than physical pain. The spiritual pain is even greater. Most ancient Near Eastern cultures could blame disease and illness on demonic activity, but because the Old Testament rejected the kind of beliefs that taught such minor gods or spirits were responsible for illness, they regarded disease as the consequence of sin. Thus they viewed physical health from both a spiritual and ethical perspective.[28]

"It was an age when ill-health, especially a serious

disorder, was not only almost universally thought of as a scourge from God, but also widely considered as a punishment for sin. Job's agony of body can scarcely be imagined by us who live in today's medicine oriented society; his agony of mind and spirit, with such views being so prevalent, must far surpass our comprehension, as he broods upon his fate." [29]

His terrible disease was eating away at his faith even more than his body. Clearly Job's comfortable and confident world had collapsed. Wealth, honor, standing and position in society, health, family—everything that gave meaning to his existence—had vanished. But even worse than that, so had much of his religious certainty. The loss of faith can be even more devastating than the loss of loved ones. Faith can get us through the death of family members, but nothing can pull us through the death of faith.

The enigmatic figure of Job's wife now makes her brief appearance in the book of Job. She comes to him and demands, "Do you still persist in your integrity? Curse God, and die" (verse 9). The Hebrew text actually says "Bless God, and die." The context clearly indicates a translation the exact opposite of what the word usually means.

But why does the wife urge her husband to choose death? Has she become the Satan's earthly counterpart? Many commentators have seen and portrayed her as a villain. Has she lost her faith and wants him to join her? Or does she have pity on her intensely suffering husband and is urging him to accept the only escape she can see from a terrible situation? As Simundson observed: "Many husbands or wives or sons or daughters have stood over the bed of their tormented loved ones and had similar thoughts." [30]

Tradition has too often treated Job's wife as a shrew. We forget that she has had overwhelming grief. She has lost her children, and her husband suffers from a painful disease. Even if she became an unwitting tool of Satan, how can we hold her completely accountable for anything she said in such a situation? The book concentrates on Job's suffering, but hers was also great.

Whatever her motivation, Job refuses to accept her suggestion. He calls her foolish and asks, "Shall we receive the good at the hand of God, and not receive the bad?" (verse 10), echoing his earlier statement in Job 1:21. Most readers take this as a pious statement of his willingness to passively accept whatever the Lord wills, but there is really here a strong recognition that God's behavior can be highly ambiguous. In fact, there is an implicit questioning of the inviolable rule of retribution in the statement that God may permit or cause evil to fall upon good people.

We cannot tell from the text what tone of voice Job used when he replied to his wife, but many commentators see here an increasing anger. But whether he spoke meekly or snapped at her, the author declares that "in all this Job did not sin with his lips" (verse 10).

Unlike in Job 1:22, however, the narrator does not state that the patriarch did not charge God with wrongdoing. As Robert Alter pointed out in his *The Art of Biblical Narrative*, [31] the slightest change in a repetition can carry deep meaning. Is Job already questioning God's justice? The Satan requested that God stretch out His hand and touch Job (Job 1:11; 2:5). The patriarch has felt His hand. Does he now regard it as a cruel hand? Has Job's loyalty to God been nothing more than blind obedience? The rest of the book will reveal the true nature of his faith in God as he struggles to understand what has happened to him.

The word of Job's calamities has spread. Three friends in particular come to visit him, some apparently from a considerable distance. Eliphaz, Bildad, and Zophar risk contagion and even guilt by association as they arrive to comfort him.

When they spot him from a distance, the disease has so disfigured him that they cannot recognize their friend in this piteous being. Their shock at his appearance startles them into performing the funeral rites as if he were already dead (Job 2:11, 12). [32] The dust drifts in the hot winds blowing off the desert. Not knowing how to respond to his great suffering, they sit in silence with him for seven days and nights (verse 13). If only they had remained silent.

---

[1] Daniel J. Simundson, *The Message of Job: A Theological Commentary* (Minneapolis: Augsburg, 1986), p. 32.

[2] Francis I. Andersen, *Job: An Introduction and Commentary* (Downers Grove, Ill.: InterVarsity Press, 1976), p. 77.

[3] James L. Crenshaw writes, "I consider these four character traits immensely significant for anyone who wishes to understand biblical ethics. The first (*tam*) indicates personal wholeness, hence integrity; the second (*yasar*) suggests that his integrity extended beyond the personal realm to the social realm. The third (*yere elohim*) characterizes Job as *homo religiosus*, and the fourth (*sar mera*) pronounces him innocent of wrongdoing. Such a one is at peace with self, seeks others' well-being, worships God with sincerity, and does no harm to fellow beings" (*A Whirlpool of Torment: Israelite Traditions of God as an Oppressive Presence* [Philadelphia: Fortress Press, 1984], pp. 58, 59, note 8).

[4] David Noel Freedman, "Is It Possible to Understand the Book of Job?" *Bible Review*, April 1988, pp. 26, 44.

[5] John C. L. Gibson, *Job* (Philadelphia: Westminster Press, 1985), pp. 5, 6.

[6] Simundson, p. 35.

[7] Good, "Job," in *Harper's Bible Commentary*, p. 410.

[8] Gibson, p. 11; A. van Selms, *Job: A Practical Commentary*, p. 24.

[9] La Sor, Hubbard, and Bush, *Old Testament Survey*, p. 583.

[10] Andersen, p. 83. Cf. Gibson, p. 12.

[11] J. Gerald Janzen, *Job*, p. 39.

[12] Habel says that the Satan's first word, ḥinnām ("for nothing"), is a direct challenge to God, while the second word, yārē' ("fear"), alludes to the concept of a wise person as one who "fears God." Ironically, the Satan is challenging wisdom theology at a point where it was often abused or misunderstood (Habel, *The Book of Job*, p. 90).

[13] Crenshaw says of the Satan that he "thinks all goodness is motivated ultimately by the reward that God bestows on virtuous people" (p. 59).

[14] Janzen, pp. 39, 40.

[15] Freedman, p. 26.

[16] "The statement is a self-curse that omits the result clause. The curse formula is, 'If A happens (or does not happen), may B happen.' Usually the 'B' clause is omitted (Job 31 presents a series of such curses, and in some, e.g., verses 7-8, 9-10, the 'B' clause is present). According to Job 1:11, the Prosecutor is willing to call down a calamity upon himself. He proposes neither a test ('Let's see if he flunks') nor a wager. The Prosecutor puts his own welfare on the line: the present clause implies the continuation, 'May something awful happen to me!' " (Good, p. 410).

[17] Crenshaw, p. 59, footnote 9; Freedman, p. 33. Freedman shows that the Old Testament has several examples of such tests.

[18] Habel sees the feast day of Job 1:13 as being simultaneous to the "one day" of verse 6 and thus coming before any likely possibility of any one of the sons "cursing God" in his heart (verse 5). As a result, Job could not interpret the disasters as the result of anything his family might have done (p. 91).

[19] The whirlwind of Palestine is only rarely what we would call a tornado, but is usually a much larger storm of wind and often rain.

[20] The reader, because of the book's concentration on Job, tends to forget about the deaths of the patriarch's children and servants. They will not share in Job's restoration at the end of the book. Their lives are gone forever. Commentators struggle with the justice of God using them as pawns to prove a point. Crenshaw particularly responds to the moral dilemmas raised by their deaths and asks why so little has been written about the apparent injustice toward them. See his *A Whirlpool of Torment: Israelite Traditions of God as an Oppressive Presence*, pp. 57-75.

[21] Some scholars see in the Hebrew word for "there" an allusion to the grave or death.

[22] In his chapter "The Techniques of Repetition," Robert Alter shows how Hebrew narrative used subtle shifts in repetition to indicate things that modern writers would need many more times the words to develop. See Alter, *The Art of Biblical Narrative*, pp. 88-113.

[23] Gibson, p. 20.

[24] Freedman, p. 31.

[25] Peter C. Craigie, *The Old Testament: Its Background, Growth, and Content* (Nashville: Abingdon, 1986), p. 227.

[26] Simundson, p. 37.

[27] For a discussion of the problem of the biblical descriptions of leprosy and other skin diseases, see Kenneth V. Mull and Carolyn Sandquist Mull, "Biblical Leprosy: Is It Really?" *Bible Review*, April 1992, pp. 33-39, 62.

[28] Gowan, *Eschatology in the Old Testament*, pp. 84-86.

[29] Gibson, pp. 20, 21.

[30] Simundson, p. 38.

[31] Alter, p. 89. See his examples throughout the chapter "The Techniques of Repetition."

[32] Throwing the dust into the air also echoes Moses' similar action in Exodus 9:10, where he began the plague of boils on the Egyptians.

The Agony of
a Dying Faith

3

THE four men have sat in silence, Job numb from agony, his three friends at a loss for words. What could one say to such a horribly disfigured man? But there was something even worse. This was their friend—they knew about his exemplary life. He was a God-fearing man. How could such calamities even happen to someone like him? Only bad people suffered like that—their religious leaders had taught them that all their lives. [1]

Could Job have possibly changed that much, that he would deserve such punishment? If he was still the good and righteous man they had always known . . . No, they mustn't think that. Such thoughts were frightening—they threatened the very foundation of their religious faith. They were the worst possible heresy. If people haven't deserved their suffering, then nothing makes sense any longer. The world is meaningless. And that is something the human mind cannot face. People would rather accept the most bizarre conspiracy theory than admit that events are nothing more than random chaos. The three friends could only cover themselves with dust—dust that drifted away in the desert wind—and look like the buried dead (Job 2:12).

Finally, the physical wreck of a man stirs and breaks the silence himself. "Let the day perish in which I was born, and the night that said, 'A man-child is conceived.' Let that day be darkness! May God above not seek it, or light shine on it" (Job 3:3, 4).

The book has now shifted from prose into poetry, apparently not an uncommon pattern in ancient Near Eastern literature. The text known as the Eloquent Peasant, for example, consists of a narrative frame and nine poetic speeches.[2] Other Egyptian texts and documents mingle poetry and prose, sometimes switching into poetry in the middle of a historical record, then reverting back to prose.[3] But none have the intensity and drama of the book of Job.

Job in his unending pain, pain that is emerging more and more as he recovers from the devastating shock of his series of tragedies, now wishes that darkness had hid the day of his birth. He may not be cursing God, but he is cursing the day that God—the One responsible for all things—brought him into the world.

Conception and birth were joyous times to Old Testament men and women as they struggled to preserve the human race for yet another generation. The people of the Old Testament desperately longed for children, especially sons, as we witness in such stories as those of Sarah and Abraham, and Hannah. They saw their immortality as tied up in their children.

The day that had made Job's parents happy, he now regarded as one of unimaginable horror. He wishes his birthday had never been. But Job is cursing more than just the day of his entrance into the world. He is calling for the complete reversal of Creation itself. Verses 3-10 take the imagery of Genesis 1 and turn it inside out. Let there be no light (verses 4-7); no time, and by implication the heavenly bodies that mark off time (verses 6, 9); no creatures of the sea (verse 8). His curse extends beyond the day of his birth to the series of images echoing the Creation story. If you call curses down upon creation, how far are you from cursing the Creator Himself?

Instead of the joyous sounds of his parents celebrating their marital intimacy (verse 7), the night of his conception should have been filled with wailing and anguish. If only the doors of his mother's womb had been locked shut (verse 10).

"Why did I not die at birth, come forth from the womb and expire?" he demands of no one in particular (verse 11). Had his been a stillbirth, he would now be resting with all those who now lie in the earth, free from ambition, strife, and labor (verses 13-19). He views here no wonderful afterlife, no harp-strumming heaven, but complete nonexistence. Only then would he be free from the physical, emotional, and spiritual pain that ravages him. Pain blown into his life by the whirlwind from the desert.

In verses 11-26 he asks a series of questions, then responds to them. They are disturbing questions, questions of a man sliding helplessly into spiritual despair—despair that will only grow worse:

Why couldn't he have perished at birth (verses 11, 12)?

If he had, he would be like kings (verses 13-15).

Why couldn't he have been aborted (verse 16)?

That would have made him like the slave who has at last escaped the torment of his cruel master (verses 17-19).

Why did he have to live when he didn't want to (verses 20-23)?

Look at what has happened to him (verses 24-26).

In Job 3:23 the suffering patriarch demands to know why God has "fenced" him in. What would he have thought about the Satan's similar complaint (Job 1:10)? God had ordered the Satan to spare Job's life, but the patriarch now saw that continued existence as only further punishment. Caught up in his agony of suffering, not being able to die and join his family in death seemed the worst thing that had yet happened to him in the strange series of inexplicable disasters that had hurled through his life.

How many millions of others have also railed in their ignorance against God's hedge about them? Will each one of us someday learn from God Himself that when we thought He had cast us into total chaos, He was really protecting us with a fence that our pain-blinded eyes could not see?

As Job concludes his verbal explosion of pain and anger, he says, "Truly the thing that I fear comes upon me, and what I dread befalls me" (verse 25). Edwin M. Good calls this "a most intriguing statement! Has his remarkable piety been motivated all along by the fear of suffering?" [4] Did God know that such fears and questions lurked in the darker recesses of Job's thoughts? Or does He recognize how far even the most mature believer has to go in his or her spiritual growth?

Job was not the only Bible individual to speak from anger and pain. Chapter 3 has many affinities with

Jeremiah 20:7-18, especially verses 14-18. How many congregations would allow their members to vent their feelings like this? God hears the pain beneath our cries of grief and anger and futility, but human beings rarely can. And Job's three friends were no exception.

Disbelief now joined their sense of shock over what had happened to their good friend. Had they heard correctly? Was this the man who had been such a spiritual pillar in the religious community?

Most of the rest of the book will be dialogue between Job and his friends. The Satan has tested Job twice, but the testing is not over. Freedman feels that the arguments of the friends are a continuation of Job's testing. Their speeches are a third attempt by the Satan to bring the patriarch down.

Eliphaz is the first to attempt a response. He means well, and he starts out kindly, with no intention of hurting his longtime friend (Job 4:2). Diplomatically, he has good things to say about Job's moral and spiritual record (verses 3, 4). But a modern counselor would suggest that he would have done better to just remain silent and let Job talk and release his pain. People in pain want a sympathetic ear, not explanations. They want someone to just share with them the loss of a child snatched from their arms by accident or terminal illness, not a theological discourse on why God saw best to let their loved one die.

Perhaps Eliphaz' biggest mistake is that he is not thinking about Job at all. As he senses that Job's religious faith is collapsing around him, that same fear seizes Eliphaz himself. It is a terrible thing to witness a spiritual pillar crumbling. Job has spiritually strengthened many (verses 3, 4). But if the faith of someone you have long admired, someone of deep wisdom and insight, can fall apart, how can your own faith possibly stand up to those same pressures and questions?

But wait—there is a way out. Maybe it's Job's fault—yes, that's it. What can we do about it?

First we must get the person to trust harder. Whip that faith into shape. Try a little spiritual pep talk (verse 6), then remind him or her of the basics, the spiritual fundamentals. "Think now, who that was innocent ever perished? Or where were the upright cut off?" (verse 7).

Eliphaz phrases his question in a way that nothing can possibly disprove the viewpoint behind it. If anything terrible happened to a person, he or she was obviously not innocent. Who can argue against such reasoning? Throughout the dialogue between Job and his friends we will see that nothing can be more dangerous than those who zealously champion partial truth.

Job's friend may have meant well, but he has committed a major blunder. First, he has implied— whether intentionally or not—that Job is obviously guilty because of all that has happened to him. Second, Eliphaz has raised the real issue behind Job's laments, an issue that Job had skirted in Job 1:21 and 2:10. The friend has based his question on the widespread idea of divine retributive justice. It teaches that God rewards righteous people with health and prosperity and punishes the wicked with calamity and suffering. To speak of the suffering of the innocent or the happiness of the wicked would be a total contradiction in terms. "If suffering is punishment for wickedness, a sign of the Deity's just handling of human affairs, there can be no undeserved suffering." [5]

Scripture solidly testifies to this fundamental religious principle, and it was the bedrock upon which not only Job's friends but also the patriarch himself built their faith. After all, what is God for if not to punish the wicked and reward the good? But what if He doesn't? What if—horror of horrors—He heaped suffering on the righteous? That was the question that was destroying Job and beginning to frighten his friends.

None of Job's friends mention the Satan. They may not have even known of such a being. Instead, Eliphaz and the others saw only two options, both based on the assumption that someone had to be wrong. It was either Job or God. Job, after carefully examining his life, chose God as the culprit, while the friends, concerned to defend God, concluded that Job had to be the one at fault.

Eliphaz decided that he had better deal with the question Job was raising as quickly and forcefully as possible. First, he gives Job his personal testimony. "As I have seen, those who plow iniquity and sow trouble reap the same. By the breath of God they perish, and by the blast of his anger they are consumed" (verses 8, 9). Eliphaz implies that Job had "plowed" iniquity and thus reaped what had happened to him. Even worse, he added that the wicked had perished from "the breath of God," "the blast of his anger," an apparently tactless allusion to the "great wind" that killed Job's children (Job 1:19). Later he will refer to the fool whose children "are crushed in the gate" (Job 5:3, 4). But Eliphaz believes that at heart Job is a good man and if he will but respond properly, he will be restored.

However, Eliphaz is not content to just argue from a shared tradition. Now he employs still another irrefutable argument—a private revelation (Job 4:12-16). During the "deep sleep" (verse 3, echoing Gen. 2:21) of some previous night, "a spirit glided past my face; the hair of my flesh bristled. It stood still, but I could not discern its appearance" (verses 15, 16). After the appropriate awe-inspiring phenomenon, a voice spoke and presented a message that Eliphaz now realizes applies to his friend Job. And Eliphaz feels threatened enough theologically that he is quite willing to use it. "Can mortals be righteous before God?" the spirit asked. "Can human beings be pure before their Maker?" (verse 17).

Where have we heard that question before? And who is the source of Eliphaz' inspiration? The question raised in heaven now echoes across the desert steppes of Transjordan. Eliphaz did not know about the kind of lying spirits recorded in 1 Kings 22:1-23, and he would definitely have rejected the possibility that such mystical experiences could even be self-induced. No, his vision was a handy club to beat Job with. If Job questioned or denied its truth, he was speaking against revelation itself. An unending line of successors have used that same claim of inspiration as a weapon to wield against their opponents or rivals.

Even the angels are not free from error, Eliphaz claims (Job 4:18, reminding one of Genesis 6:1, 2 and perhaps Psalm 82:1, 2, 6, 7). If the angels can fail so badly, what can one expect of mere mortals (Job 4:19-21)?

Eliphaz has already contradicted himself in his speech. At first he held out the possibility that Job could be restored if he reshaped his life (verse 6). Now he categorically states that all human beings are spiritual failures. Simundson suggests that Eliphaz' argument that all human beings were imperfect in God's sight was an attempt to make sense of God's justice without really being too hard on his friend, [6] but it still hurt deeply.

In Job 5:1 Eliphaz argues that it is futile to even pray for help because no one will answer. Verses 2-7 spin a series of vivid images of the fate that awaits the "fool" who behaves like Job has. (A study of the uses of the various words for fool in the book of Proverbs will hint at some of the jabs Eliphaz was making at Job. Sadly, though, Job has employed an even stronger word for fool against his own wife in Job 2:10.)

These images echo Genesis 2:7 and 3:17-19 (still another indication of the many affinities between the two books). And they portray human beings as helpless and hopeless creatures (Job 5:7).

Finally, after verbally stomping Job into the ground, Eliphaz grandly announces, "As for me, I would seek God, and to God I would commit my cause" (verse 8). He recites a series of illustrations of how God helps the lowly and needy, and frustrates the plans of the wicked (verses 9-16). Yes, God does that, as Scripture frequently testifies, but does He do it every time? Does it apply to Job's case? Furthermore, is life really that simple?

Finally Eliphaz comes to his point. If Job will just listen to him, everything will be all right. "How happy is the one whom God reproves; therefore do not despise the discipline of the Almighty" (verse 17). If children can rebel against a simple discipline such as spanking, how could Job possibly rhapsodize over what he has gone through? What kind of God would kill one's children and countless loyal and devoted servants just to teach Job a lesson or two?

But such questions do not trouble Eliphaz. He is terrified that Job's experience might prove his religious understanding wrong. He rushes on with a list of wonderful things that God will do for Job if he will but respond properly to divine discipline. God wounds and strikes, then His hands bind up and heal (verse 18). Nothing really harmful would touch him.

Unfortunately, Job believes that he has felt the touch of that hand, and it had seemed anything but a gentle one. In verse 21 Eliphaz tells Job that God will hide him from the scourge of the tongue, and the patriarch may have wished that He would immediately deliver him from his pious friend.

Eliphaz concludes with an idyllic description of Job's life if he will just recognize that the most effective medicine is often the most bitter tasting, and say, "Thanks, God, I needed that." He will then be at peace with the predators that prowled the hills and deserts of Palestine (verses 22, 23), fear nothing from marauders and thieves, and have "offspring like the grass of the earth" (verse 25). In time, after a ripe old age, he would come to his grave "as a shock of grain comes up to the threshing floor in its season" (verse 26). [7]

One can imagine Eliphaz standing there, perhaps with a loving smile on his face and evangelistic appeal in his voice, as he gestures at the other two friends and says, "See, we have searched this out: it is true. Hear, and know it for yourself" (verse 27).

But how can he say such things? Job's wealth has been stolen and all his children are dead. And although he would like to die, he can't—God cruelly keeps him alive.

Eliphaz has begun a pattern that he and the other friends will persist in following. Job laments his grief and pain, but they want to argue theology. He asks for comfort, and they try to straighten out his doctrine. They hear nothing of what he is really saying; both Job and the friends will speak past each other from now on. The friends know nothing of what is going on in Job's life, yet they have judged him and backed him into a corner, where he feels driven to defend himself. Theological dogmatism never heals pain. The dialogue between Job and his friends will only get more cruel. It is as much a part of the Satan's testing of the patriarch as the disasters and the disease.

---

[1] The Old Testament teaches this concept repeatedly, but perhaps nowhere more eloquently than in Psalms 37 and 73.

[2] Miriam Lichtheim, *Ancient Egyptian Literature: A Book of Readings. Volume 1: The Old and Middle Kingdoms* (Berkeley, Calif.: University of California Press, 1973), pp. 169-184.

[3] Some examples include the record of the Asiatic Campaigns Under Pepi I, the Hymn of Victory of Thutmose III, and the Hymn of Victory of Me-ne Ptah (the famous Israel Stela). See Pritchard, *Ancient Near Eastern Texts*.

[4] Good, "Job," in *Harper's Bible Commentary*, p. 411.

[5] *Ibid.*, p. 412.

[6] Simundson, *The Message of Job*, p. 52.

[7] Ancient Israel did not always regard death with the horror that we do today. Frequently Old Testament Scripture speaks from the perspective "that death in itself is no great tragedy, to be puzzled over and protested, but is to be accepted as the normal conclusion of a long and fulfilled life" (Gowan, *Eschatology in the Old Testament*, p. 90). Only later would they begin to understand more clearly that death was really an enemy.

The Price of Integrity

4

ELIPHAZ has interpreted Job's cries of grief and lament as nothing more than bad theology and even heresy. Instead of healing his friend's emotional and spiritual wounds, he has opened them more. The whirlwind from the desert was devastating, but nothing compared to the words that will blast in gales of anger and fear from the lips of his friends.

The patriarch now replies to Eliphaz. As Edwin Good puts it, "Job's second speech is a wild, stream-of-consciousness spray of confusing, contradictory images, as if it depicted a man trying to think in the throes of pain." [1] And that is what Job's words will be all the way through the poem. He wants to tell them how much he hurts, and his friends want to straighten out the theology they think they hear him espousing.

Job feels that his suffering and pain is beyond measurement, although he acknowledges that what he said has been "rash" (Job 6:2, 3). But he believes that he has good cause for acting as he did because "the arrows of the Almighty are in me; my spirit drinks their poison" (verse 4). God Himself has been attacking him. It is no longer a suspicion or fear, but a growing certainty.

He has had plenty of time to look deep into his heart, and while he knows he is not perfect, still he has

51

done nothing of the magnitude that would deserve what has happened to him. Since he accepts the fundamental religious tenet that God is in control of everything, Job concludes that the Lord has to be responsible for his suffering. God is punishing him for absolutely no reason at all. The patriarch's integrity is the fundamental issue of the whole book.

In verses 8-13 Job repeats the desire to die that he brought up in chapter 3. While he has "not denied the words of the Holy One" (verse 10), he realizes that he is reaching the limits of his ability to cope with all that has happened to him (verses 11-13). And one thing in particular is pushing him over the edge—the way his friends have responded to his grief.

Although only Eliphaz has spoken so far, Job lashes out at all three for withholding the kindness he so desperately needs (verse 14). He compares them to the wadis, or dry riverbeds, of the Near East that will course with water during the rainy season or while the winter snow and ice melts, then disappear during the dry season (verses 15-17). The trading caravans heading north from the Arabian peninsula will spot such wadis—perhaps still green with vegetation from the vanishing moisture—and hope to obtain water from them, only to be disappointed when they find no permanent spring, and possibly perish (verses 19, 20). The Hebrew of verse 21 is extremely difficult, but apparently means that his friends have been like such wadis to him.

Verses 22 and 23 list a series of requests that he denies ever having asked. Simundson sees them as Job's recognition that they cannot make the pain of his suffering go away.[2] Francis Andersen wonders, "Is Job saying that, since he is not indebted to them for anything, he can speak his mind freely? Do we have here the pride of a man who has always paid his own way, and even now, in dire need, will not even take advantage of friendship, with a request on which a shade of a question might fall?" [3]

Perhaps Gibson summarizes Job's intent when he says, "It was not as if he [Job] had been asking them for money! He had not been begging them for a loan or for help to cross an important person's palm (then as even now, it seems the way to get things done in the East: see Isa. 1:23; Micah 3:11). Nor had he been imprisoned for debt, or kidnapped and a large redemption price or ransom slapped on his head which he wanted them to pay for him. All he was asking for was a little human sympathy, and they didn't want to know him." [4]

They reacted with such hostility not only because they saw in him a threat to their religious worldview, but also because of the fear that always surfaces when we encounter someone who is suffering. As an experienced chaplain observes, we struggle with a number of problems. "What are we going to say? We want to speak a word that will be helpful. We wish we had the power to make the pain go away. We wonder how we will respond to the hard 'Why?' questions. We know we have no good answer and we are afraid that we will look stupid or helpless. . . . We don't have any easy answers, any miracle solution, any power to change things." [5]

Job has done nothing to warrant the deaths of his children and loyal servants, let alone the loss of his wealth. Can't his friends understand that? "Teach me, and I will be silent; make me understand how I have gone wrong" (Job 6:24) he begs. Honest words will always have a powerful impact on any person: "But your reproof, what does it reprove?" (verse 25). Do they consider what he has said out of his desperation as little more than wind (verse 26)? (Wind—what a frightening allusion to that whirlwind from the desert.) Job is becoming increasingly conscious of the issue of his guilt.

Angrily he charges that his friends would even stoop to gambling over an orphan so they could sell him into slavery to pay off his father's debts (verse 27). The biblical world enjoined the community to take special care of the orphan (for example, Exodus 22:22, 23; Deuteronomy 10:18; 24:17; Isaiah 1:17; James 1:27), and to mistreat or take advantage of the "fatherless" was considered a particularly grave social crime.

The friends, insensitive as they might be, hardly deserved Job's insults. After all, they had come long distances to visit him during an age when travel was difficult, and they had already spent a week sitting with him. His complaints, tirades, and accusations would hardly fit into most religious people's definitions of blamelessness and uprightness. But God understood.

Using a legal oath—"I will not lie to your face"—Job urges the friends to reconsider their view of him (verse 28). Desperately wanting vindication (verse 29), he argues that surely he must know whether he is telling the truth and when he is experiencing calamity (verses 29, 30). As Edwin Good points out, Job now echoes Eliphaz' understanding of how suffering must follow wrongdoing.[6]

Job 7:1-6 compares life to that of slavery under a cruel taskmaster—and God is that taskmaster. At night he can't wait for dawn, and during the day he longs for darkness to come (verse 4). Verse 5 shows the powerful impact a physically suffering body can have on the mind and the religious outlook. Where before life had been joyous, now the disease ravaging his body made him feel like a slave enduring the days that fled past with the rapidity of a weaver's shuttle (verse 6).

His horror and misery build up until he explodes in a mixture of bitterness, and frustration, and cries for help to God Himself (verses 7-21). He reminds God that his life is fragile, and when he dies God will no longer see him (verses 7, 8). Like a vanishing cloud in the dry desert sky, human beings disappear into death—Sheol—and never return (verses 9, 10). Or to put it another way, Job's life is but a puff of wind. Again we see no joyous expectation of some wonderful afterlife. Job does not have the sense of immediate entrance into heaven claimed by many Christians.

His sense of pain and desperation forces him to speak (verse 11). This is ridiculous, God, he says. "Am I the Sea, or the Dragon, that you set a guard over me?" (verse 12). The sea and the dragon were well-known symbols of the forces of chaos in the ancient world. Not only did the pagans portray their gods as battling such agents of disorder, but also the Bible writers used the same symbols, even though they did not believe these entities really existed. They merely employed them as modern man uses political symbols (see, for example, Exodus 14; Psalm 18:15; 74:12-14; 89:9, 10; Isaiah 17:12-14; 27:1; 30:7; 50:2; 51:9, 10; Ezekiel 29:3-6; Nahum 1:3-5; Habakkuk 3:8, 10, 15; Mark 4:35-41; and, of course, Revelation 12 and 13).[7]

What Job is saying here is "God, am I as powerful as

these symbols of evil and chaos that You have to keep attacking me? I'm no threat to You. So why do You treat me as though I were?"

The patriarch protests that God won't leave him alone. The Lord won't even let him sleep but deliberately terrifies him with nightmares and visions to the point that he would rather be strangled than live on (verses 13-15). "Let me alone, for my days are a breath" (verse 16), he protests again.

Verses 17 and 18 are a bitter parody of Psalm 8. Job turns the thoughts of the psalm upside down. In verse 19 he asks God to look in the other direction and ignore him at least long enough for him to swallow his spit. He doesn't want the intensity of attention that Psalm 8 says God devotes to humanity.

By verse 20 the patriarch openly acknowledges sinfulness and guilt. (Even the upright and blameless can be troubled by self-doubt.) But what importance is it to God that He has to react so drastically? Why does he, Job, have to be such an all-consuming divine target? Why has he become such a special obsession to God? Why can't God just pardon him, take away his transgression, and get it over with? After all, Job will soon die and be no more. Not even God will be able to find him then (verse 21).

Implicit in Job's argument is a concept frequently expressed in the book: "that God is too high to be affected by men's actions, whether sinful or righteous." [8] However, God is anything but impassive or indifferent to His human creation. Christians regard the cross as the greatest demonstration of the effect both humanity and its sin have on God. He loves the men, women, and children He created, and He demonstrated that love by dying to save them.

Scripture teaches that He intimately and deeply feels our every joy and hurt. Our tears are His, our pain anguishes Him. And He revealed His horror at the terribleness and alienation of sin by the fact of that same death. Jesus wept over the death of Lazarus (John 11:35). His words at the cross "My God, my God, why have you forsaken me" (Matt. 27:46) portray the impact sin has on the divine sensitivity.

But even apart from the New Testament, the Hebrew scriptures emphatically declare that God is not distant and aloof, but feels intensely toward us. [9] In the Old Testament He personally visited Abraham and summoned Moses into His presence. Constantly He agonized over His people and creation.

But Job was right about one thing. He was not God's target because of any sin that he had done. And this idea greatly disturbed and threatened the next of Job's friends to speak.

If Eliphaz began with a conscious attempt at tact and consideration, Bildad plunges into the dispute. Perhaps he is reacting in shock to the violence in Job's attacks on God, or perhaps he feels that he must take more drastic measures to force the patriarch to see the error of his ways and position.

"How long will you say these things, and the words of your mouth be a great wind?" (Job 8:2), he probably shouted, perhaps again painfully reminding Job of the death of his children from the "great wind" that had howled in from the desert. "Does God pervert justice? Or does the Almighty pervert the right?" (verse 3), Bildad demands. Once Job would have emphatically answered no along with him, but now he is not sure.

Then Bildad makes the cruelest statement so far. "If your children sinned against him, he delivered them into the power of their transgression" (verse 4). The ancients viewed things in a more collective or corporate sense than do modern Westerners. What the members of a family or clan did affected the whole group for good or bad. Job bears the guilt of whatever his children did, and thus must share in the punishment they brought upon their whole clan. Could Bildad have said anything more devastating to a father who conscientiously offered sacrifices for his children lest they sin? But people who feel their religious beliefs threatened will do and say anything.

Seek God, Bildad urges. Pray and make supplication to Him. If you will return to purity and uprightness, then He will restore you, and you will be even more prosperous than you were before (verses 5-7). Bildad's approach to God echoes that of the Mesopotamian world. When suffering, disease, or tragedy struck, the victim automatically assumed that he or she had done something to displease his or her god. It was time for repentance.

Unfortunately the gods spoke only to the priests, and then only in general and vague ways. The average person had no way of finding out how the Deity had been offended. [10] So he or she would resort to a general, all-purpose ritual of repentance. One might recite something like the following:

"I profanely took a solemn oath in your name,
I profaned your decrees, I went too far.
I promised and then reneged: I gave my word but
then did not pay.
I did wrong, I spoke improper things,

> I repeated . . . [what should not be uttered];
> improper things were on my lips.
> I spoke lies, I pardoned my own sin." [11]

Job's friends treated repentance as "a panacea and universal solvent." [12] They thought one should repent whether one could think of a reason or not. But for Job to have repented here would be to play into the Satan's hands by questioning his own integrity and relationship with God.

Unlike Eliphaz' speech, in which he acknowledged Job's past upright life, Bildad's is filled with a series of nasty "ifs." Also, Eliphaz had said that all human beings were sinners, while Bildad implied that God responds only to the upright. They contradicted each other in some ways, but they were united in their belief that Job had to deserve his suffering lest his case shatter their own religious underpinnings.

To support his theological assertion, Bildad appeals to tradition. No single individual lives long enough to test the theological principle of retribution, but the experience of many generations shows that it is so (verses 8-10). In the words of Simundson: "If our own experience seems to contradict what we have been taught, we should be hesitant to throw out the wisdom of the ages on the basis of our limited perspective. Truth that has lasted for centuries cannot be dismissed casually as if the experience of one individual can offset what has been acceptable teaching by a large consensus over a long period of time. This is particularly true for teaching which has hardened into sacred doctrine." [13]

The problem with most of the arguments that Job's friends make is that they contain much truth but don't apply to every situation—especially Job's. As Freedman observes about the type of reasoning behind both their conclusions and Job's interpretation of his experience, "The premises may be correct, and the logical reasoning impeccable, but the inferences may still be quite wrong." [14] God will never pervert justice (verse 3), but how can they prove that fundamental principle applies to Job's case? Much theological controversy stems from people trying to apply theological teachings to inappropriate situations. Both Job and his friends believe in the doctrine of retribution, but only Job can sense that his case might be an exception.

In many ways we can sympathize with the friends. For example, most of us have lived long enough to realize that Psalm 37:25—"I have been young, and now I am old, yet I have not seen the righteous forsaken or their children begging bread"—is a wonderful statement of God's care and love, but simply does not apply to every situation in life. Yet we would rush to the passage's defense if anyone questioned or attacked it. How and when do we recognize when situations change or other principles apply?

Using a series of images from nature—the favorite source of insight and instruction in wisdom literature—Bildad attempts to demonstrate the certainty of God's justice (verses 11-20). The wicked only appear to prosper for a time, but that prosperity has no more solidity than a spider's web (verses 14, 15). They may thrive like plants in a garden, but after the gardener pulls them up they will vanish as if they had never been (verses 16-18).

Perhaps mentally calming himself, Bildad manages to close with a few phrases of reassurance for Job. If he will repent of his evil and become blameless again, God will accept him (verse 20), and once more Job will laugh and shout for joy (verse 21). Those who hated Job (perhaps an allusion to those who might have mocked Job in his suffering and losses) will be covered with shame and "be no more" (verse 22). With the "be no more" Bildad may be picking up on Job's "I shall not be" of Job 7:21.

Repent—that is the recurring theme of the friends' speeches. But Job can't do that. To repent under these terms would be to admit that he deserved his suffering and thus to play into the Satan's hands. Even the Satan has agreed with God that Job is a just and upright man, and the patriarch must do nothing to support the false claims the accuser has made about him.

The Satan wants to break Job down and destroy the relationship he has with his God. If he could do that, the accuser would win the test. In the words of David Noel Freedman, for Job to repent the way his friends want him to would be to "seek cheap grace at the price of his innocence and integrity. . . . For Job to throw in the towel would prove Satan right and God wrong about Job." [15]

As is so often the case with theological argument, Job's friends are forcing him by partial truths into a corner that has no escape.

---

[1] Good, "Job," in *Harper's Bible Commentary*, p. 412.

[2] Simundson, *The Message of Job*, p. 54.

[3] Andersen, *Job: An Introduction and Commentary*, pp. 132, 133.

[4] Gibson, *Job*, p. 61.

[5] Simundson, p. 54.

[6] Good, p. 412.

[7] For a more detailed discussion of this ancient imagery, see Foster R. McCurley, *Ancient*

Myths and Biblical Faith: Scriptural Transformations (Philadelphia: Fortress Press, 1983), pp. 12-71.

[8] Victor E. Reichert, *Job*. Revised by A. J. Rosenberg (London: Soncino Press, 1985), p. 32.

[9] Jewish writers, although accepting only the Hebrew scriptures, constantly portray God's feelings toward and love for humanity. As just one example, consider Abraham J. Heschel's classic work, *The Prophets* (New York: Harper and Row, 1962).

[10] The fact that the God of Israel revealed so much about Himself was one reason that the psalmist and other biblical writers could declare, "Oh, how I love Your law!"

[11] Quoted in Walton, *Israelite Literature in the Cultural Context*, p. 155.

[12] Freedman, "Is It Possible to Understand the Book of Job?" *Bible Review*, April 1988, p. 27.

[13] Simundson, p. 57.

[14] Freedman, p. 44.

[15] *Ibid.*, p. 28.

Shouting at God

5

BILDAD has tried to get Job "to grovel before Bildad's forgiving God when he can see no reason in his own conduct why he should." [1] Job launches into a new defense of himself, a speech that is filled with difficulties for the modern translator because of rare and ambiguous words and obscure phrasings. Many translators have attempted to solve the problem by emending the text, that is, changing the words or word order so that an obscure passage will make more sense.

Ancient written Hebrew consisted only of consonants. Writing was, in a way, more of a memory aid than an independent form of communication. The reader filled in the vowels because he knew the word and text, and spelling in the Biblical world was much more regular than it is in English or even many other modern languages. Deciphering the sentence "Cn y rd ths?" will give you an idea of what they had to do. Also, spacing between letters and words on manuscripts might not be clear if the ink was faded or smudged (biblical scribes used a half letter space or a dot between words), so our sentence might then appear like "Cnyrdths?" Fortunately, the roots of Hebrew words consisted of groupings of three consonants, and a trained scribe could get along quite well.

But a modern reader has a more difficult time reading ancient manuscripts, since he does not know the text as well, especially in the case of rare words or obscure allusions. The translator can substitute different vowels in an attempt to make sense out of a passage. The "rd" of our example could be "reed," "read," "rood," "rude," "ride," or many other combinations, though what we can read clearly elsewhere in a text would naturally rule out many possibilities. Also, the translator might try breaking or adjusting the letters into different groupings. Thus "God-isnowhere" can be either "God is nowhere" or "God is now here." [2]

Because Joban scholars face many problems like this throughout the book, commentators will sometimes disagree dramatically on what a section such as chapter 9 is saying. The ancient versions in Coptic, Greek, and other languages as well as the Targums or Aramaic paraphrases give some clues to how to translate parts of the book, but their great diversity shows that translating the book was difficult even centuries ago. Despite their growing knowledge of ancient languages and study of ancient texts, scholars still struggle with the text of Job. For example, is Job being sarcastic here, as some argue,[3] or is he being reverent? [4] But we can get enough to catch the general sense or drift of what the author was trying to say.

Though Job's speech follows that of Bildad, in Job 9:1-10:22 he is really replying to Eliphaz. Job begins with a near quotation of Eliphaz' statement in Job 4:17, though he may be using it in a different sense.[5] He asks, "How can a mortal be just before God?" (Job 9:2). Clearly he is not raising the same type of question that

Martin Luther had in mind—he is not talking about salvation. Rather it is, How can a person possibly think of arguing with God (verse 3)? No one has ever succeeded in resisting Him (verse 4). God is infinitely wiser and more powerful, as Job illustrates through a series of nature and creation images (verses 5-13) that echo Job 38. But the creation images of chapter 9 are turned upside down. God does not bring order out of chaos, as He did in Genesis 1, but here the Deity angrily makes disorder (see especially verses 5-7). Job is afraid of God and realizes that the Divine Being is beyond comprehension or even perception (verse 11). Thoughts of creation do not lead him to hymnic praise but to terror. Who would dare accost such an awesome and terrible Being and demand, "What are you doing?" (verse 12)? Even worse, God will ask questions Himself. In an ironic prophecy of what will actually happen, Job groans that no matter how innocent he might be, he will be unable to answer God (verses 14, 15; cf. chap. 38-41).

Throughout chapter 9 we find imagery based on the law court and the artisan's workshop.[6] Job longs to put God on trial—and though Job does not realize it, knowing nothing about the heavenly assembly, God is indeed on trial through Job. The Satan has made accusations against Job that are really directed against God Himself. The question the Satan hurled at God about the motivation behind Job's allegiance to Him also raises the issue of what kind of being the man worships. God stands on trial before the sons of God—and by implication the whole universe—but the patriarch cannot see beyond his own search for justice.

"Job continues to use courtroom imagery to describe his present relationship with God. He stands convicted, as demonstrated by the suffering with which he is afflicted. Somehow he must convince God that he is really innocent. But how can he do that? The system is working against him. How can he get a fair hearing from the one who is his accuser (verse 15)? Job believes that God has brought his troubles upon him (verses 17, 18). Therefore, God is not impartial toward Job. A judge is supposed to approach a case with an open mind, but God has already decided about Job. So God acts as both prosecuting attorney and judge. And there is no way to bring God into account, no supreme court to whom an appeal can be made, no way to force God to listen to the case (verses 16, 19)." [7]

Caught up in his suffering, oblivious to what has been going on in heaven, Job can see only a divine whirlwind of destruction bearing down on him. There is no way out. Even though in his heart and soul he knows that he is innocent, he fears that if he should have a chance to speak to God, his own mouth would condemn him. In Job's mind God has become a monster who would twist everything to "prove me perverse" (verse 20). But there is worse yet to come.

Job has had a long time to think now, and his friends' words have been triggering thoughts that truly frighten him. Eliphaz claimed that no innocent person had ever perished (Job 4:7) and Bildad argued that God would never "reject a blameless person" or help the wicked (Job 8:20). But when Job looked deep into his own experience, he could come to only one horrible conclusion. God not only permits calamity to strike the innocent (Job 9:23), but turns the world over "into the hand of the wicked" by blinding justice (verse 24). "If it is not he, who then is it?" the patriarch agonizes. [8] And God will never tell him. Job will die with his question unanswered. Only the reader knows the part the Satan has played.

Sitting on the village dustheap, surrounded by friends who bring only more pain instead of comfort, Job feels his life fleeing past (verses 25, 26). If he tries to cheer himself up and to think positive thoughts, he believes that he will be struck by still more suffering. Why? Because "I know you will not hold me innocent" (verses 27, 28).

What's the use of it all? Even if Job tries to clean himself up, God will plunge him into greater filth (verses 30, 31). It will be centuries yet before Zechariah sees in vision the Satan bring still another accusation against someone. The prophet will then learn that God does not defile, but actually cleanses (Zech. 3:1-5).

God is divine (and, Job believes, also corrupt), while Job is a mere mortal; there is no way there could ever be a trial between them (Job 9:32). The Lord can do whatever He wants and get away with it. Now, if only there were an umpire between them "who might lay his hand on us both" (verse 33).

The Pentateuch contains two dramatic accounts of someone interceding for another with God (Abraham for Sodom in Genesis 18:22-33, and Moses for Israel in Exodus 32:7-14; cf. Deuteronomy 9:13, 14). In each one the human being changed God's intention, but Job does not seem to know the stories. He views God as too hostile toward him to withhold punishment, so he feels that he needs someone much more powerful.

Francis Andersen explains that the Hebrew word *môkîh* does not mean a judge who merely decides who is in the right, but rather "a mediator who settles the quarrel by reconciliation, a negotiator who brings both parties together, by *laying his hand upon us both* as a common friend. This interpretation is more natural than the idea that Job is thinking of some power greater than God who could 'impose his authority on us both.' " [9]

By chapter 10 Job has reached such a state of frustration and bitterness that he again declares life not worth living (verse 1). But he still wants to know why God has brought such suffering upon him. After telling God to stop condemning him and to let him know what charge He has brought against him, Job hurls a series of questions at Him (verses 3-7). Some commentators sense a sad nostalgia in these questions, a longing for the good old days.

Job asks if God derives some kind of human pleasure out of hounding him (verse 3), or if He just sees things from a different perspective (verses 4-7) than a mortal would. [10] Do You understand, God, what it's like to be human? the patriarch wonders. Or it might be that God doesn't have time to catch Job in sin, so invents a reason before he escapes His clutches. [11] The patriarch reminds God that He created and took care of him, so how can He mistreat him like He has been doing (verses 8-12)? Doesn't God have any respect for His handiwork, of which mankind is the greatest? It just doesn't make sense.

In verses 16 and 17 Job feels like the prey of a hungry lion or the target of military attack. Then in verses 18-22 he again wishes that he had never been born, that he could escape to the darkness of death. While previously death had appealed to him, now it seems far less attractive. [12]

The patriarch continues his argument against God—but why does he? It's as if he cannot give up on the Lord. Do we usually keep on arguing with someone who we expect will never respond to us? Most of us will either retreat into silence or aggressively break the relationship. But Job hangs on—he won't let go of his Creator. Is the man still hoping that the Deity will vindicate Himself, that He will somehow show that despite all appearances to the contrary the world is still one of order and love? That the relationship they formerly had can once more resume? The loss of God overwhelms him far more than the destruction of his wealth or even the death of his children and servants.

Emotionally and spiritually exhausted, the suffering patriarch finally lapses into silence. But Zophar is ready to leap into the fray. As he has listened he has grown even more shocked and impatient at Job than were Eliphaz and Bildad. When Job pauses, Zophar attacks, determined to defend God and orthodox theology and to straighten out his complaining friend once and for all.

Should Job's nonsense go unanswered? he sputters. How dare the patriarch think that anything could ever possibly vindicate him (Job 11:2). Why are people letting him silence them when they should expose him for the shameful thing he is (verse 3)?

Job may claim "My conduct is pure, and I am clean in God's sight" (verse 4) [13] Zophar says, but if God should speak, Job "would see how far superior divine wisdom was to human. Job had refused to accept the verdict of human wisdom that his afflictions proved him to be a sinner but, confronted with divine wisdom, he would realize that God was in fact letting him off lightly." [14]

Zophar "has seen Job's hostility toward God, his lack of trust in God's justice, and his exaggerated claims for innocence. By these reactions in his time of trouble, Job has begun to show what kind of person he really is. There is no reason any longer to be kind to a person who says God laughs at the calamity of the innocent and has given the world over to the hands of the wicked (Job 9:23, 24). God is just and Job is a sinner and all is right with the world." [15]

The angry friend grills Job with a series of questions (Job 11:7-9) that foreshadow chapters 38-41, [16] but they reach a far different conclusion. They illustrate the complex mixture of truth and error in the minds of all of Job's friends. In verses 10 and 11 Zophar shouts that God knows iniquity when He sees it, and will not let people get away with it. [17] Repent, put away your iniquity, [18] and everything will be all right, he insists (verses 13-19), taking many of Job's words and turning them against the tortured patriarch. [19] But death is the only escape for the wicked (verse 20).

To use a person's own agonized cries against him or her is an especially cruel thing. But in the defense of what he believes is truth, Zophar is willing to employ any tactic that might give him an advantage. Traditional religion was more important to him than even the pain of his friend. And Zophar still has many heirs today.

---

[1] Gibson, *Job*, pp. 74, 75.

[2] Ancient Greek manuscripts and texts employed no spacing between words and sentences, but Hebrew usually gave some indication of word breaks. However, there are a few cases in which confusion appears to have arisen over how the scribe was to separate the

consonants into different words. According to Alan Millard, the best example is Amos 6:12, where if one breaks the Hebrew *bqrym* into *bqr* and *ym*, the passage preserves its parallelism and makes better sense. See his "Were Words Separated in Ancient Hebrew Writing?" *Bible Review*, June 1992, pp. 44-47.

[3] For example, Gibson, p. 75.

[4] Andersen, *Job: An Introduction and Commentary*, p. 145.

[5] Good, "Job," in *Harper's Bible Commentary*, page 413, suggests that Eliphaz had morality in mind, while Job is here talking about law.

[6] Janzen, *Job*, p. 89. The artisan imagery is used of God's creation. Jerry Gladson says, "Legal language . . . appears throughout his speeches (cf. chaps. 6:29; 9:15-19, 32, 33; 13:3, 13-16, 22). In chapter 31 Job concludes with an oath of innocence, an ancient legal declaration of guiltlessness. He tries, in short, to 'sue' God!" (*Who Said Life Is Fair?* p. 49).

[7] Simundson, *The Message of Job*, p. 59. Ironically, as Crenshaw points out, "Job has no case at all against God apart from an operative principle of reward and retribution, for in a world devoid of such a principle good people have no basis for complaining that the Creator has abandoned the helm and thus allows the ship to wander aimlessly amid submerged rocks" (Crenshaw, *A Whirlpool of Torment*, p. 62). Job is thus both arguing from the perspective of retribution—one which he shares with his friends—while at the same time rejecting it because he believes with his whole heart that he does not deserve the kind of suffering he has gone through. His experience shows the kind of mental anguish we all go through because of our limited understanding of God's ways and the complexity of the struggle between good and evil.

[8] "Job moves very quickly from seeing God as amoral to accusing Him of immorality. . . . Only God can be the subject of that astounding statement. He is not merely amoral but so 'wicked' that He does away with His own kind" (Good, p. 413). This is the man God called blameless and upright.

[9] Andersen, p. 151.

[10] *Ibid.*, p. 153.

[11] Gibson, p. 90.

[12] Simundson, p. 61.

[13] Nowhere in the text does Job really appear to claim such a thing.

[14] Gibson, p. 97.

[15] Simundson, p. 62.

[16] "That raises some questions for us to keep in mind as we continue to look at the book of Job. If Job accepts this word from God at a later time, why cannot he accept it from Zophar now? It must have something to do with the timing (perhaps it is too early for Job to abandon his search for answers) and with the relationship between Job and the one giving the advice. It is one thing to be told by God Himself that human beings are incapable of penetrating all the mysteries of life and death and God. It is another thing to be squelched by an anxious peddler of a rigid doctrine who knows that his position cannot withstand too many critical questions and so he pulls out the ultimate conversation stopper: 'It's all a great mystery and therefore we cannot discuss it' " (*ibid.*, p. 63).

[17] Verse 11 has also been translated in the sense that God will ignore iniquity because it is not worth His bother or attention. See Andersen, p. 158.

[18] Zophar has little understanding of the power of sin in the human personality. As Edwin Good comments: "How can Zophar so lightly propose (verses 13, 14) that Job just 'prepare [his] heart' and 'if guilt is in your hands, send it away'?" (p. 414).

[19] Janzen, p. 99.

Who Gets the Blame When Things Go Wrong?

―――――――――― **6** ――――――――――

ZOPHAR'S taunt that Job has received less punishment than he really deserves (Job 11:6) jolts the patriarch into a temporary composure. In his next response Job will be calmer than he has been for some time, though he is not above sarcasm when he tells Zophar "wisdom will die with you" (Job 12:2). "But I have understanding as well as you," he adds. "Who does not know such things as these?" (verse 3).

Eliphaz, Bildad, and Zophar had come to comfort him, but something went terribly wrong in their mission. "I am a laughingstock to my friends," Job cries in pain. "I, who called upon God and he answered me, a just and blameless man, I am a laughingstock" (verse 4). The friends must have winced as they heard him refer to himself as "just and blameless." How could he possibly still believe that? Doesn't he recognize beyond any possible doubt what his suffering indicates?

As Job remembers the time when he could pray and God would answer, he contrasts it with the way the world as he has known it has turned upside down. Those free from suffering tend to treat those experiencing it with contempt (verse 5), but he now knows better. In verse 6 Job appears to imply that making one's own power the object of ultimate concern can become a form of spiritual idolatry.

The friends feel secure in the wisdom tradition of their world and time, but Job is becoming aware of its limitations. The world is in God's control and He can do with it whatever He wants—things often beyond human understanding (verses 7-25). Echoing Job 1:21, he says that God gives and God takes away, whether in nature (verses 15, 22) or in human affairs (verses 17-21, 23-25). His graphic illustrations remind the reader of the language of the psalms, and verse 9 parallels Isaiah 41:20. One finds true wisdom, he argues, not in age and length of days but in God (verses 12, 13).

Although Job is correct in emphasizing the superiority of God's wisdom, a fundamental principle of the book, he quickly gets sidetracked. Once again one of the human beings in this cosmic drama has become obsessed with God's power to the exclusion of everything else. Instead of divine power being a source of comfort, it frightens Job. No one can ever oppose God (verse 14), he gasps, because even history is under His inscrutable control (verses 23-25). But Job, trapped in a worldview that regards suffering as only punishment, cannot see in his pain that God is more than naked power or wisdom. It takes all of revelation—especially those aspects of God's character demonstrated by the life and death of Jesus—for us to see the broader picture. He is also love and mercy and justice and a host of other attributes that always temper that power.

After again reminding the friends that he is their theological equal and they should not talk down to him (Job 13:1, 2), Job repeats his desire to take his case directly to God (verse 3). But first he lashes out at their disastrous failure as comforters. "Worthless physicians," they "whitewash" Job's situation with lies on behalf of God (verse 4). They would have been much wiser to have just kept silent (verse 5). Though they may have lied to make God's case look better—when they really should have been on Job's side—they will not escape when God gets around to judging them (verses 7-10). Then, terrified by His majesty (verse 11), they will find that their maxims were "proverbs of ashes" and that their defense of God was nothing more than "clay" (verse 12).

The friends have been doing what religious people always do to those who threaten their theological understanding—attack the person who raises the theological problem instead of trying to resolve the problem itself. Writing from his experience as a hospital chaplain and pastor as well as a scholar, Simundson asks, "Why do we always blame the human beings when things go wrong and even deny the message of our senses in order to protect God's reputation? Why do God's counselors feel they must rush in to defend God from the outlandish cries of a despairing human being? Who needs more comfort in a situation like that—God or the poor human being? Job would contend that God can take care of Himself. Job needs an intercessor to stand up for him before God. His friends should be less concerned with defending God and more interested in comforting Job. Instead of comfort, he feels condemnation. Even the truth becomes distorted, e.g., they must try to make Job out to look like a heinous sinner—in order that God might be protected." [1]

The questions Job has raised are disturbing ones. His pain has probably made him phrase them even sharper than he need have. No matter how one brings them up, however, they disturb religious sensitivities. But can anything excuse how Job's friends have treated them? How do we treat those we might consider to be opponents of God and His church? Do we unwittingly slip into sarcasm and character assassination in order to undermine their teachings or positions? Are we so concerned about God and truth—sometimes only our particular understanding of truth—that we are willing to resort to anything that might demolish their beliefs? Are we tempted to use any argument as long as it works? Would we distort and misrepresent to gain an advantage?

Even Job has not escaped what he accuses his friends of. God will eventually have to reprimand him for doing the same thing in his own defense (Job 40:8), but at least the suffering patriarch has more excuse than does Eliphaz, Bildad, or Zophar. From now on we will see Job and the friends talking past each other, the inevitable result of theological controversy that values being right more than it does people.

Job 13:13-28 again reveals the patriarch torn between two conflicting emotions. One part of him recoils in horror from the growing conviction that God is attacking him, while another part clings to the hope that God will not only vindicate him (verse 18) but also God Himself.

Job announces that no matter what the possible consequences, he is determined to make his case before God Himself (verses 13-15). He believes that he can approach God unafraid because he is innocent (verse 16). Verse 15 has raised problems because most modern translations have abandoned the traditional translation "Though he slay me, yet will I trust in him" (KJV). The NRSV renders it, "See, he will kill me; I have no hope; but I will defend my ways to his face," with a footnoted reading of "Though he kill me, yet I will trust in him." [2] But in verse 18 he declares, "I know that I shall be vindicated," and in verse 19 he asks, "Who is there that will contend with me?" The latter two verses suggest that however we should translate the passage, he has not lost all hope.

Having only barely acknowledged their existence in this speech, Job turns from his human friends to God Himself and requests two things that he had earlier asked in chapter 9:34—for God to withdraw His hand from him, and to stop terrifying him (verses 20, 21). If God will do that, he will speak to Him (verse 22; cf. Job 9:35).

Job wants to meet God at the city gate (the ancient site of justice) and settle once and for all why God is now acting as his enemy. It doesn't matter who starts first, but two questions need to be resolved: What has Job done wrong, [3] and why is God now hiding His face from someone who had once been so close to Him (verses 23, 24)? [4]

In verse 25 Job conjures up the astounding image of the God of the universe chasing him like some wind-blown leaf or a bit of dry chaff. Is Job really that important that God must devote so much time and effort against him and ignore His duties of running the rest of creation? Yet, ironically, Job was right in the sense that he was indeed occupying the center stage of

God's attention. The patriarch was the focal point of the universe as the heavenly assembly watched Job respond to his suffering. Was God or the Satan correct about his character and motivation?

If God is finally dealing with the indiscretions of his youth, Job now suggests, then God is rather late and bitterly overdoing it (verse 26). The patriarch feels like a prisoner put into stocks and accompanied by his jailer as he hobbles on his limited round of exercise (verse 27), and like a rotting or moth-eaten garment (verse 28).

In chapter 14 he repeats ideas and concepts that he has expressed previously, but he does so in what has been considered one of the greatest poems in all of literature. His brief flash of hope in chapter 13 vanishes into the darkness of the spiritual storm raging around him. The poem's images of the fleeting human condition echo such other biblical passages as Psalm 90:5-17, Psalm 103:15-18, and Isaiah 40:6-11, but Job fills them with more despair and pessimism. The winds of suffering have blown away much of his hope and sense of God's loving presence. When things start going bad for us, it is an instinctive human reaction that God is after us, even though our reason and faith tell us otherwise.

"Who can bring a clean thing out of an unclean?" he asks in Job 14:4, then answers himself, "No one can." If only God would leave such miserable creatures as himself alone and let them live out their brief existences in peace.

During his prosperous days Job rarely thought about his mortality. Now he is acutely aware of the shortness and uncertainty of life. Even worse, he struggles with the question of whether the present life is all there is. He alternates between hope and despair.

In verses 7-9 he grasps the illustration from nature that a tree that has been cut down will cling to life by sending up new shoots, though it may not regain its full height or size. [5] But in verses 10-12 doubt threatens to overwhelm him as he compares human life to water evaporating during drought or the summer dry season of Palestine.

Job wishes that God would hide him in Sheol [6] until the Deity has gotten over His inscrutable anger, and then remember the patriarch and summon him forth once more (verses 13-15). [7] Job has only a rudimentary understanding of the doctrine of resurrection. That would come in its fullness later. Here the suffering man must cling to God without a full awareness of the possibilities of an afterlife.

But a glimmer of hope does shine through. And it depends on God alone. "All Job's hopes are summed up in the belief that God will *remember* him (verse 13). God's thought names people into real existence and remembers them from continued being. Job as creature has no existence, in fact or detail, except in the continued willing of his Creator. Here is no doctrine of immortality as an intrinsic and inalienable property of the soul. For any person to live is ever the act and gift of God." [8]

Not only does Job hope to be remembered back into existence by God, but also that the Lord will do something about whatever his sins and transgressions might have been (verses 16, 17). The mention of a bag may be a reference to the kind of practice recorded in cuneiform tablets from ancient Nuzi and elsewhere. Merchants took pebbles placed in a shepherd's pouch and transferred them to various receptacles to represent the actual movements or changes in status of the animals being counted. [9] Also, the owner of a flock or herd might put the same number of pebbles or clay symbols in a bag as the number of animals he sent out with the herdsman. If Job has something like this in mind, then he is saying that God will seal up the record of his transgressions forever.

It is an inescapable fact of suffering that anyone caught up in it continually swings back and forth from hope to despair; and Job is no exception, as we see in verses 18-22. As the heavy winter rains of Palestine wear away the mountainous landscape by washing away the soil, so God destroys hope. Men and women die and know nothing of the fate of their children. [10]

Even the most wonderful glimpses of hope may not prevent the exhausted and pain-filled human mind from slipping back into gloom and discouragement. A decision of the human will does not magically vanish grief and sorrow. We can only choose whether we will let our pain or God rule our lives, and Job is still caught up in the struggle of that decision.

Job and his friends have now gone through one round or cycle of speeches and responses. The friends now begin a second series. They will present few if any new ideas, but will amplify the charges and accusations they have already made. Like most of us, they assume that by repeating themselves often enough, they will get through to Job and convince him of the truth of their position and the error of his own. Sadly, both they and Job will often start out with sarcasm.

Since Eliphaz has not been able to rebut Job's claim that he did nothing to deserve such suffering, he dismisses everything the patriarch has said as "wind," or in a modern English idiom, "hot air" (Job 15:2). The image of wind seems to haunt Job. Wind from the desert killed his children, he compared Eliphaz' earlier first speech to wind (Job 6:26), and now the friend throws the comparison back at him, specifically alluding to the east, or desert, wind. The east wind fills the air with a haze of dust, withers the vegetation, and physically exhausts human beings.

Eliphaz, through his dismissal of everything Job has said as nothing more than "windy" words, is rejecting Job's understanding of his experience and thus is rejecting the patriarch himself. But Eliphaz feels driven to do so because, as he tells Job, "you are doing away with the fear of God, and hindering meditation before God" (Job 15:4). Job's claim that God is unfairly punishing him is threatening not only traditional religious doctrine but something else as well: Job's right to continue complaining to God.

"Ancient Israelite piety saw no contradiction between fear of a powerful God and willingness to complain about what that God did to them. Both were central elements of the concourse between humans and Deity. Eliphaz seems to worry that, because Job is unacceptably guilty, he may undermine his religious freedom to complain. Job is becoming the prosecution's star witness in this trial. Every word he speaks ensures a guilty verdict." [11] "Your own mouth condemns you, and not I; your own lips testify against you" (verse 6).

Simundson suggests that Eliphaz also worries that "if God really is unjust, as Job has been saying, then the simple faithful folk would lose their motivation for being obedient to God's commands and ordinances. If

Job had his way, nobody would fear and love and serve God anymore." [12] In other words, Job, don't raise questions, because it will upset the average member. It is but one example of the same vicious arguments still used in theological controversy.

In verses 7 and 8 Eliphaz raises a challenge similar to one that God will bring against the patriarch in Job 38:4 and 36. But Eliphaz couples with it the type of argument we slip into when all others have failed: "Do you think you're better than us?" (cf. verse 9). Tradition and intelligence are on our side, he claims in verse 10.

By verses 11-13 Eliphaz resorts to such arguments as "Isn't the way God does things good enough for you? He's treating you better than you deserve, [13] having chosen us to help you. Why are you rebelling against Him? Your every word is blasphemy."

Beginning to run out of ideas, he repeats the theological doctrine of chapter 4:17-21 and echoes the parody of Psalm 8 that Job made in chapter 7:17. Eliphaz argues that God finds everyone less than Himself contemptible, especially Job "who drinks iniquity like water!" (verses 14-16).

Finally, perhaps not knowing what else to say, he uses the argument of last resort. He concludes his speech by threatening Job with hellfire and damnation (verses 17-35). However, he has the wicked receiving their punishment in this existence, not some afterlife. They writhe in pain (verse 20), hear terrifying sounds and face destruction at the height of prosperity (verse 21), fear the dark (verse 22), and wander about in a desperate search for food (verse 23).

John Gibson suggests that Eliphaz defines a wicked man as one "who would 'play the hero' (verse 25; RSV has 'bids defiance')," or challenge God Himself. Naturally such brazen impertinence will bring Job internal turmoil and anxiety. "Marked down for the sword, destined to be hunted and plundered, he will become the victim of unceasing alarm and fear. And his dread will not be misplaced. Declared an outcast from decent society, he will make no enduring wealth and sink no permanent roots. Like a tree burned by fire or blasted by the wind, he will be destroyed and thus fully requited for the vanity of his ways, and the godless and mischievous company he keeps." [14]

Unlike Eliphaz' first speech, his second does not contain any word of encouragement for Job. He has given up trying to humor the patriarch. Theological controversy does this to friends. The issues being fought over become more important than friendship or any other relationship.

---

[1] Simundson, *The Message of Job*, p. 65.

[2] Gibson observes, "The received Hebrew text contains the word *lo*, spelt in this way to mean 'not'; but the margin (what the scholars call the Masoretic notes; the Masoretes being medieval Jewish scribes and textual experts) has the same word spelt slightly differently, so as to give the meaning 'to, for, in him.' We may compare this with English homonyms like *son* and *sun*, or *bare* and *bear*. The modern versions follow the text, arguing that, in this passage, Job is conjuring up courage out of the depths of despair, and that to have him suddenly changing gear in midstream and confessing trust or hope in God, would be to diminish its defiant force. He is appealing to a God who is treating him as though he was his enemy (verse 24), and appealing magnificently, but in his innermost being he knows that he will not be given a hearing" (*Job*, pp. 110, 111).

Further Gibson points out that the verb translated as "trust" by the KJV usually has the basic meaning of "wait" in the book of Job, as we see in such passages as Job 29:21; 30:26; and 32:11, 16.

But he concludes that while the KJV does perhaps overstate what the text says, "Nevertheless, we ought to see in this verse something more than despair. This nuance of 'something more' can be imparted even to *lo*, ie 'not,' by adding the adjective 'other,' as the Jerusalem Bible does ('I have no other hope'). But it can be even more effectively achieved through a combination of the reading *lo*, 'for him,' and the translation 'wait.' Although Job does not at this point look beyond his own death, the seed of the thought is planted in his mind which will be expressed out loud in 14:14, although it will then, before the speech ends, be swallowed up once again in melancholy. I suggest the following free translation for verses

WHO GETS THE BLAME WHEN THINGS GO WRONG?

15-16:

"Though he slay me, yet will I wait for him.

Only I must be able to defend my conduct before him.

That is the only way I shall be saved,

since no hypocrite would dare to approach him" (*ibid.*, pp. 111, 112).

Simundson suggests that Job is saying, "Even if God kills him, there is no other hope" (p. 66). Balmer H. Kelly, in *The Book of Ezra; The Book of Nehemiah; The Book of Esther; The Book of Job* (Atlanta: John Knox Press, 1962), holds that Job sees his hope "*beyond this life*" (p. 86).

[3] Gibson feels that Job is admitting that he has done something wrong and sincerely desires to know its extent. "This may be because he is convinced that the answer will convict God of punishing him more than he deserved, that it will show God's treatment of him to be quite out of step with anything he could have done to offend Him. But at least he is, if belatedly and indeed temporarily, abandoning his pretense of perfection, and looking askance at his former way of life of which so far he has been so inordinately proud. The balance sheet is, for the present, no longer all black on God's side and all white on Job's" (pp. 115, 116).

[4] Speaking of the biblical image of God remaining silent or hiding, Crenshaw says, "An eclipse of God often accompanied behavior that stank in the divine nostrils. The Old Testament abounds in threats of divine withdrawal if the people does not change its ways, and this explanation for divine silence occurs over and over. A hiding face implies anger, but it suggests even more than this. The departure of the deity means that time is being granted during which reconciliation can take place. Or it implies that God has simply given up on the individual or nation who brought on the act of concealment" (*A Whirlpool of Torment*, p. 64).

[5] However, cf. Good, "Job," in *Harper's Bible Commentary*, p. 415: "The Hebrew Bible has no expectation of a pleasant afterlife, and the analogy to the tree has a rueful tone."

[6] Gibson points out that where sick or suffering people plead in the psalms for deliverance from Sheol, they are really asking for God to rescue them from an early death. In Psalm 116:8, 9 the speaker goes to the Temple to thank God for such deliverance. But Job knows that while nothing can stop his approaching death, he yet hopes that God will hear him someday. It appears as if Job almost accepts that he is guilty of something, but believes that God will forgive his transgression. Gibson feels that a closer parallel is Psalm 139:8, where the psalmist believes that even if he is in Sheol, God will still somehow find him there, contrary to the idea presented in Psalm 88:10-12, that God did not interfere in Sheol. But there is still little or nothing of the later biblical understanding of resurrection or an afterlife for the redeemed (pp. 122, 123).

[7] Andersen suggests that not only does Job see the grave as a temporary hiding place, but also that "it is another period of contracted *service*" (*Job: An Introduction and Commentary*, p. 172).

[8] *Ibid.*, p. 173.

[9] Gaalyah Cornfeld, *Archaeology of the Bible: Book by Book* (San Francisco: Harper and Row, 1976), p. 212. Cf. Klaas A. D. Smelik, *Writings From Ancient Israel: A Handbook of Historical and Religious Documents* (Louisville: Westminster/John Knox Press, 1991), pp. 5, 6. The use of clay tokens or symbols as a means of recording information may be the earliest form of writing. See Denise Schmandt-Besserat, *Before Writing* (Austin: University of Texas Press, 1992). This work consists of two volumes. Volume 1 is titled *From Counting to Cuneiform* and volume 2 *A Catalog of Near Eastern Tokens*.

[10] Several scholars see in chapter 14 a chiasm, or inverted parallelism. Verse 22 would be the reflection or mirror image of verse 1. Thus verse 22 would not be talking about the dead feeling pain, but an echo of the trouble endured by mortals in verse 1. Janzen suggests that Job's body, "on its way back to the dry dust of death, pains him," and the hope he had in

83

verses 7-9 now dies (*Job*, p. 110). We can only mourn in life, not death.

Chapter 14 presents a very different attitude toward death than that contained in the Egyptian document known as "The Dispute Between a Man and His Ba." The narrator longs for death so he can be resurrected according to Egyptian religious belief with its concept of a comfortable and enjoyable afterlife (see Lichtheim, *Ancient Egyptian Literature*, pp. 163-169). Job does not desire death as a doorway into a wonderful new existence. Instead, he sees death as oblivion.

[11] Good, p. 415. Cf. Gerald Wheeler, *Footsteps of God* (Boise, Idaho: Pacific Press, 1987), pp. 27-29.

[12] Simundson, p. 75.

[13] If Eliphaz intends irony in verse 11, he is being terribly insensitive. But if he is serious, it is even worse. "To think that God is both consoling and gentle with Job is to refuse to experience the real world" (Good, p. 416).

[14] Gibson, p. 129.

Cosmic Spotlight

7

BY NOW Job and his friends are experts at hurling each other's words back in their faces. Job calls all three friends "miserable comforters" (Job 16:2), the same word rendered "mischief" in Job 15:35. Eliphaz had said that Job was full of "wind" (Job 15:2), and Job sarcastically tells him he does not expect Eliphaz' "windy words" (Job 16:3) to stop. Although God has called him blameless and upright, Job is a real person with real human emotions. He is hurting, both from what appears to be God's attacks on him, and from the treatment he has received from his friends. The patriarch is no plaster saint.

Stating that so far he has heard no new insights from his friends (verse 2), Job adds that he could also string platitudes and proverbs together like they have been doing (verse 4). If he were in their sandals, watching someone else suffer instead of enduring the pain himself, he would feel as wise and comforting as they did (verse 5). But whether he speaks or remains silent, his pain will not go away (verse 6).

While the friends have been doing their part to make his life miserable, Job still believes that it is really God who has been attacking him. He uses an explosion of imagery to describe the divine campaign against him. God has worn him out (verse 7), torn him and gnashed His teeth at him (verse 9), and thrown him into the hands of the wicked and ungodly (verse 11). His divine Adversary breaks him in two, dashes him to pieces (verse 12), and uses him for target practice (verses 12, 13). The divine Warrior launches campaign after campaign against him (verse 14) [1]—all despite the fact that "there is no violence in my hands, and my prayer is pure" (verse 17). But God is not the only one to shatter his life—human beings have done their part also (verses 10, 11, 20).

In verse 18 Job makes still another allusion to the book of Genesis: the murder of Abel by Cain (Gen. 4:1-16). Job wants his blood to cry out unceasingly for vengeance, just as Abel's did (Job 16:18). Then he declares, "Even now, in fact, my witness is in heaven, and he that vouches for me is on high" (verse 19).

And who is Job's witness? God Himself. "Though crushed by God, he still turns to God as his only hope. Though temporarily overwhelmed by the image of God as violent enemy, Job has not entirely lost what he once knew about God. He appeals to that earlier vision of a God who is compassionate and merciful and just, the God he used to know back in the good days before all the trouble started. Maybe that God will hear his pleas and make his case for him with the other God who has been hurting him. Job, of course, still believes in only one God, but he is torn by his different perceptions of God. At the same time, God is both enemy and also the only chance for vindication, redemption, deliverance." [2] Job wishes that God would come to his aid as a neighbor would in a legal dispute at the village court by the city gate (verse 21). But he sees only death awaiting him (verse 22; Job 17:1).

The patriarch's speech is now a terse string of images and arguments. His argumentation and meaning have puzzled not only modern readers but even the ancient copyists and translators.[3]

What Job believes that God has been doing to him is bad enough, but the reactions of his fellow human beings to his suffering add even more to his incomprehensible load of pain. He is surrounded by mockers (verse 2) and people who denounce friends for reward (verse 5);[4] anger and deep hurt mingle with his grief. (Later, in chapter 30, he will vent his frustration over the treatment he received from people who turned against him when he was down.) In verses 3 and 4 he demands that God do something about such people, asking for a pledge that the Deity will defend him.

Then immediately his mood swings in another direction. Job cries that God has made him "a byword,"[5] and one whom people spit at in contempt (verse 6). What has happened to him appalls the upright (verses 8, 9), though some commentators see Job as saying that the morally pure turn against him instead of defending him.

Andersen interprets this passage as Job being "outraged because he, the man after God's own heart, has made matters worse for himself by maintaining his own integrity. He has laid himself open to the charge of hypocrisy on top of secret sin."[6] Gibson sees verse 10 as a defiant challenge for his friends and those of like mind to resume their attack on him and to do their worst.[7]

As Job spiritually thrashed about in his pain, he felt that he would be a "byword" of contempt and derision, but instead he became the human symbol of endurance and ultimate hope. Until Christ brings an end to all suffering, God's people will cling to James's reassuring words, "You have heard of the endurance of Job, and you have seen the purpose of the Lord, how the Lord is compassionate and merciful" (James 5:11).

The patriarch's name became a byword of hope to the suffering of all generations and a witness to the entire universe. Job may have ranted and sobbed and wanted to strike out at both Deity and humanity, but despite everything that had happened to him, he could not let go of the God whom he begged, "Lay down a pledge for me with yourself" (Job 17:3).

Job 17:11-16 is still another passage of difficult Hebrew, but "it is clear that Job is convinced that there is no longer any hope for restoration for him within this life. Though his comforters speak as if there may be 'light at the end of the tunnel' (verse 12 may mean something like that) if Job repents and turns his life over to God, Job is convinced that there is nothing ahead of him but death, Sheol, the grave, and the worms that will eat his flesh (verses 13, 14). There is no hope—either for this life or for anything after this life has ended. If the best you can look forward to is a family consisting of the grave as your father and worms as your mother and sister, then you are indeed in a sad state."[8]

The grave was not an automatic portal to some higher plane of existence, a gateway to some angelic paradise. Instead, it has become a barrier to seeking God.[9] And Job is driven to find God, even though the Deity terrifies him.

Simundson summarizes chapters 16 and 17 by saying that "Job has virtually hit rock bottom."[10] But he is still God's servant, unknowingly defending God's trust in him.

Bildad now returns to the theological fray. Job's comments about his lack of wisdom have stung him (Job 18:3),[11] and his attack becomes even more personal (verse 4). Because he is rigidly loyal to the tradition of retribution, and Job's experience does not fit into his black-and-white worldview, Bildad's frustration and fear begin to almost border on demonic hatred. He can only think, *Job, God's going to make you pay for this!*

He accuses Job of thinking that the world revolves around him, that he is the cause and focus of some cosmic dilemma. He snarls, "Shall the earth be forsaken because of you, or the rock be removed out of its place?" (verse 4). Yet—irony of ironies—Bildad is right. Unknown to the four men sitting there at the dung heap, the heavenly assembly and the universe it represents are watching them and their theological disputes. God is indeed concerned about Job's suffering.

But like countless men and women engaged in theological controversy, Bildad can see only a man whose torment is obviously a punishment from God on someone who refuses to accept responsibility for whatever he has done. Job is impiously rejecting his undeniable guilt.

The rest of his speech Bildad spends in outlining the terrible fate of the wicked (verses 5-21). He catalogs every terror he can think of, ranging from fear to disease to hunger, though he is especially obsessed with the fate of those who die without descendants or leave no historical memory behind (verses 17-19).

Does Bildad have in mind the death of Job's children? He illustrates how too often those enmeshed in theological controversy cannot resist the temptation to attack the person when they do not know how to respond to his or her ideas or experience. And attack at a particularly painful and sensitive spot—the loss of the patriarch's children. Because Job won't admit that he is guilty and deserving of all his suffering, thus preserving the traditional theological understanding, Bildad is determined to unleash a storm of threats on him that will blow some sense into the patriarch. The storm that roared in from the desert and smashed the house of Job's children will be but a gentle zephyr in comparison to what awaits Job if he does not repent.

As Andersen forcefully reminds us: "Bildad's description of the fate of the wicked is academic. He does not think how horrible it must be to be God, doing such things to helpless men, however justly. He does not stop to think how horrible it must be to be a man suffering such things, whether justly or unjustly. Bildad recounts the disasters as the outworking of moral laws which control the movements of men around the central God as gravitation governs the movements of planets around the sun. God's justice consists of His maintenance of these laws, natural and moral. This is a common opinion of philosophers, whose god is a factor in a formula." [12]

Yet at the same time, we must recognize that Bildad was a sincere man concerned about protecting the faith of his people. A guardian of his religious heritage, he meant well—but he was wrong. Job was not a threat to his religion, but its greatest human demonstration of its ultimate truth. Although Bildad charged that "wicked" people like Job would fall into a trap and snare (verses 8-10), the angry friend was actually the one to find himself caught in a far more dangerous snare. His zeal without love, his incomplete understanding of God and religion, and his blind adherence to tradition transformed him into a tool of the accuser. Before anyone dares to defend the faith, he or she must know what the real threats are. And those threats are rarely the human beings we see suffering around us.

Bildad concluded his description of the fate of the wicked with "such is the place of those who do not know God" (verse 22). He believed that he understood God and had the better relationship with Him, but events would prove that Job was the only one that really knew the Lord. While Job was God's servant, Bildad had become the slave of the Satan.

---

[1] Job borrows the concept from Eliphaz (Job 15:25-27), where the friend had the wicked mounting a military assault against God. Job now turns the image around and portrays God as personally attacking him. God as celestial warrior fighting for His people appears in such passages as Exodus 15:1-6; Psalm 28:8-10; Isaiah 29:5-8; and Revelation 19:11-16. Instead of battling for His people, defending them, conquering for them, He now selects one individual—one of His most loyal—and launches a campaign against him for no reason at all.

[2] Simundson, *The Message of Job*, pp. 79, 80.

[3] A. van Selms, *Job: A Practical Commentary*, p. 68.

[4] Moffatt translated the verse to state that people around Job were "like one who bids friends to a feast and lets his children starve!"

[5] "The Hebrew word translated 'byword' in the RSV is used in other places to indicate the judgment that will come upon the people of Judah when God sends them into exile (e.g., Deut. 28:37; 1 Kings 9:7; 2 Chron. 7:20; and Jer. 24:9)" (Simundson, p. 80).

[6] Andersen, *Job: An Introduction and Commentary*, p. 185.

[7] Gibson, *Job*, p. 141. A. Cohen suggests a similar thought, having the patriarch tell his three friends, "Renew your attack on me . . . take up your stale arguments, if you like, deriding me for what has come upon me. You will only expose the more your unfeeling folly" (*Job* [Soncino Press, 1950], p. 88).

[8] Simundson, p. 80.

[9] Gibson, p. 141.

[10] Simundson, p. 80.

[11] Bildad addresses someone in the plural (verses 2, 3). It could either be a mistake in grammar or, as some have suggested, he could be speaking to Eliphaz or Zophar as well as Job, thus hinting at a breach among the three friends who had come to comfort the suffering patriarch.

[12] Andersen, p. 190.

Engraved Testimony

---8---

JOB'S first reply to Bildad was rather short. Apparently the patriarch did not think it worthwhile to respond to his friend's defense of traditional religion. But the barbs in Bildad's second speech, especially what he had to say about God, struck deep into Job's spirit, and it was almost more than the patriarch could bear.

Job's friends see him no longer as a person, but as a theological abstraction. They do not sense his pain or feel compassion for him. Something happened in their hearts out there on the dustheap. Now it is as if they must destroy him to protect their theological faith.

"How long will you torment me, and break me in pieces with words?" Job cries (Job 19:2), repeating Bildad's opening comment. The three friends have repeatedly defamed his character and should feel ashamed at what they have done to him (verse 3). And if he has erred, if his theology is wrong, then he alone must bear responsibility for it—not them. He is no threat to them—has not really bothered anyone—and they have no right to use his disease and other humiliation as an argument against him (perhaps by flaunting their own healthy bodies). Job's problem is strictly between him and God (verses 4-6).

The patriarch responds in ever-increasing anger to

his friends, because anger is one stage of the grief process, and he is deeply grieving over his great losses. First we deny in our grief our pain and loss, then we become angry over it. Anger results from an overpowering sense of helplessness. Disaster after disaster has pummeled Job and taken away almost everything that has given his life meaning, and there is no way he can fight back, no way he can stop or remedy the loss. He feels that God has grabbed him by the scruff of the neck and will not stop shaking him. Who can possibly fight or even resist God?

His friends refuse to hear what he is really trying to say, no matter how hard he tries. All the frustration builds and builds until he can hold it back no longer; he explodes in anger. God understands his reaction—after all, He made Job—but human beings rarely do. To really comfort someone, we must accept the person's anger for what it is—an inevitable stage of grief—and at the right time help the person channel the energy into nondestructive outlets. But reacting to a sufferer's pain and loss by arguing theology—as Job's friends did—will only generate more anger.

In verse 7 the word "violence" has the connotation that the word "rape" would have in modern society. Using this word was supposed to summon help for the weak. But no one came to Job's defense, especially the heavenly Judge who had been ignoring the cry of the patriarch's innocent blood. [1] If God would not rush to his aid, how could he possibly expect his human friends to side with him?

Job feels that God hems him in on every side, dethrones him like a captured king, besieges him as an enemy (verses 8-12). Or is it, he desperately hopes, just

His army, not God Himself who has launched the attack against him (verse 12)? Friends, family, and servants have turned against him (verses 13-19). His wife recoils at the stench of his diseased breath (verse 17), and the village children ridicule Job (verse 18). The relationships that gave meaning to life have vanished as all those he has known now reject him, and he is barely surviving (verse 20).

"Have pity on me, have pity on me, O you my friends," he begs in desperation, "for the hand of God has touched me!" (verse 21). All he asks for is some human comfort, but they have instead behaved like the demon God who seems determined to consume him (verse 22). Perhaps if they had been God's comforting human hands, the touch he thought he felt from God would not have been so painful.

The suffering patriarch does not want his defense of his integrity to vanish with his death. He hopes that someone will either preserve them in a written document (a scroll or clay tablet) or engrave them on rock (verses 23, 24). Rock inscriptions dot the landscape along the ancient caravan routes in Sinai and Arabia (graffiti is nothing new), and rulers carved inscriptions on cliff faces. Job wants his testimony cut into rock and then the letters filled with lead to make them stand out more clearly.[2] In that way Job will have a kind of immortality. Carved words would not be forgotten. The Egyptians carved the Pyramid Texts and the Egyptian Book of the Dead—incantations to protect and preserve them in the afterlife—on tomb walls lest the priests at the mortuary temples forget to continue the sacred rites.

Verses 25-27 contain some of the most familiar

words of the whole book, especially verse 25, but as modern translations indicate either in the text or the footnotes, we are not sure what all the Hebrew words mean. Different translators often approach the passage in quite different if not even contradictory ways. [3] In fact, as Edwin Good comments, "Nearly every interpretation of these lines rests on a scholar's proposal to rewrite some point of them." [4] But despite all the problems and uncertainties, there are some things that we can be sure about. First, let us look at how the NRSV translates verses 25-27:

"For I know that my Redeemer [or *Vindicator*, footnote] lives, and that at the last he [or *that he the Last*, footnote] will stand upon the earth; and after my skin has been thus destroyed, then in [or *without*, footnote] my flesh I shall see God, whom I shall see on my side [or *for myself*, footnote], and my eyes shall behold, and not another."

Simundson summarizes the role of the *go'el*, translated here as "Redeemer," explaining that "in Hebrew tradition [the *go'el*] is the next of kin who performs certain acts on behalf of a relative who is not able to take care of them himself, usually because of death. For example, the redeemer (*go'el*) may be the one who avenges the blood of a family member who has been murdered (as Num. 35:19-21; see Job 16:18, 19), or who buys back property that might otherwise be lost to the family because of debt (e.g., Lev. 25:25), or who marries a widow in order to provide the deceased man with descendants (e.g., Boaz in the book of Ruth; see also Mark 12:18-27). Sometimes there seems to be no hope for a human being who will step forward to take the part of the next of kin in these situations, and God

Himself is implored to become the 'Redeemer,' the 'Avenger,' the 'Vindicator.' This same Hebrew word is used to describe God in Psalms 19:14 and 78:35, in Jeremiah 50:34, and several times in Isaiah (including 41:14; 43:14; 44:6, 24; 47:4; and 48:17)."[5]

The root concept of *go'el* is that of "the avenger of blood," as we especially see in Numbers 35:19 and Deuteronomy 19:6, 12. If one emphasizes the avenger role, the passage could imply little more than that someone will avenge Job after his death has been caused by God, or that Job's *go'el* actually intensifies the hostility the patriarch feels must exist between him and God.[6] But concentrating on other aspects of the *go'el* figure will suggest a more favorable fate for Job, one that actively involves God in Job's deliverance.

Job's friends have not offered to vindicate him, nor could they have even if they had wanted to. They are as powerless before the Deity as Job. Only God can be *go'el* to Job.

Translations that appear to downplay the concept of the bodily resurrection in Job 19:26, 27 also bother many readers of the Bible. While the biblical doctrine of the resurrection does not stand or fall on this passage, yet even in the difficulties of this passage a number of things stand out that support it. They include:

1. That Job will in some way "see" God. Three times the two verses mention the concept of seeing. Furthermore, he will have the experience not as a disembodied spirit but as a physical being. While many modern translations downplay here the idea of resurrection in the flesh, seeing, for example, that God will champion or vindicate Job after his death when his body is nothing but dust, others, such as J. Gerald Janzen,[7]

argue that the concept of resurrection is fundamental to what Job is proclaiming here—that though Job swings between proclaiming and denying it, he does uphold it in verse 25.

2. That God will be the one who acts as Job's *go'el*, or Redeemer. Even a Jewish commentary such as that by Cohen in the Soncino series, while naturally rejecting any connection with a Being such as Christ, acknowledges that verse 25 teaches that Job believes that God is on his side. [8]

3. That there will be a permanent record of the patriarch's innocence. The book of Job is itself such a record. It is a far more eternal one than even words carved in rock.

Job then closes his speech with what seems to be a warning to his friends that God will hold them accountable for the way they have treated him (verses 28, 29), especially for insisting that his suffering is his own fault—"The root of the matter is found in him."

Naturally Zophar cannot let Job's warning go unanswered. Listen to me, he shouts. I've got to answer you or I will explode (Job 20:2). The noun translated "thoughts" implies disturbing and anxious reflection. In addition, he feels insulted (verse 3). Perhaps, as Balmer H. Kelly suggests, he has "temporarily wavered in his dogmatism," but having "crushed down any unsettling thoughts," he returns "to the safety of the absolute principle set out in verses 4 and 5." [9] The wicked don't last long—that's the way it has always been, and that's the way it always will be.

What he says has truth in it. But it is only partially true—because it simply does not apply to Job's case. Here we have one of the greatest dangers of quoting from the book of Job. Everyone except God speaks only partial truth because of his finite knowledge and perspective, and God Himself deals only with certain aspects of Job's situation. Even all of Scripture gives us only limited and selective glimpses of God's ways and of the cosmic struggle between good and evil. We will spend eternity in God's presence learning more and more.

For the rest of the chapter Zophar will orate on how the wicked meet their fate. One can imagine him becoming more and more caught up in his list of the horrors awaiting evildoers until he is actually shouting at his suffering friend. They well up from him so fast that he doesn't even realize that he contradicts himself, as we see when we compare verses 21 and 22. In the one verse the wicked have nothing to eat, while in the next they have everything their appetites could desire. Theological controversy and anger do not worry about logic and consistency. Only exhaustion must have stopped his catalog of doom as he—perhaps out of breath—finally gasped, "This is the portion of the wicked from God, the heritage decreed for them by God" (verse 29).

---

[1] Crenshaw, *A Whirlpool of Torment*, p. 71.

[2] Some have suggested the Copper Scroll found at Qumran as an example of what Job might have had in mind. Another example would be the so-called Gezer calendar, a text about the planting seasons apparently scratched as a scribal writing exercise on a piece of limestone (see Klaas A. D. Smelik, *Writings From Ancient Israel: A Handbook of Historical and Religious Documents*, pp. 21-28). The Israelites, however, rarely carved inscriptions on stone or metal. Instead they wrote with ink on plastered surfaces (for example, Deuteronomy 27:1-4). The Balaam inscription found at Deir Alla in Jordan illustrates the type of thing they would have done. See André Lemaire, "Fragments From the Book of Balaam Found at Deir Alla," *Biblical Archaeology Review*, September-October 1985, pp. 26-39.

[3] Andersen says the passage has "several lines which are so unintelligible that the range of translations offered is quite bewildering" (*Job: An Introduction and Commentary*, p. 193).

[4] Good, "Job," in *Harper's Bible Commentary*, p. 418.

[5] Simundson, *The Message of Job*, p. 86.

[6] Good, p. 418.

[7] Janzen, *Job*, pp. 135-145.

[8] Cohen, *Job*, p. 99.

[9] Kelly, *The Book of Ezra; The Book of Nehemiah; The Book of Esther; The Book of Job*, p. 103.

Painful Reality

9

JOB now answers Zophar, not from the viewpoint of
the traditional doctrine of retribution that all four
men share, but from the painful teaching of everyday
experience. While doctrine should reveal more than
what such daily experience can teach us, at the same
time it must not contradict it. The harmony between
doctrine and life as we constantly experience it may be
on a deep and possibly even hidden level, but it must
be there.

The patriarch begins his reply less emotionally than
his previous experiences. He asks his friends to listen
carefully and bear with him (Job 21:2, 3), though he
cannot resist a sarcastic "then after I have spoken,
mock on."[1] The suffering man offers reasons that he
has been impatient and observes that he understands
their reaction because even he is appalled at his
appearance and condition (verses 4-6).

Francis Andersen points out that the speech is
unusual because it is the only time Job does not resort
to either a soliloquy or a prayer. Instead, he will meet
their theological position head-on. As he does so, he
goes over much of the preceding discussion "so that
many cross-references can be found to what has
already been said. These are a valuable guide to
interpretation when they can be discovered. . . . By

quoting their words and refuting them, Job comes nearer to formal debate. While his words are still emotional, there is less invective in them."[2]

Naturally the friends refuse to accept Job's claim that his problem originates not with him but with God, and totally without cause or reason. But even Job is "dismayed" (verse 6) by the new concept he is struggling with. It violates every principle and sense of order and meaning that has guided his life until now, and he finds himself whipped about by a spiritual whirlwind of chaos. It is said that an earthquake is so frightening because the ground—the symbol of all stability—suddenly violates that security. Job's spiritual life has gone through an even more traumatic experience.

In his speech Job will now propose a viewpoint that is the exact opposite of his lost spiritual stability. He is boldly questioning the doctrine of retribution (though he will never fully give it up) despite the fact that it undergirds his religious beliefs. The patriarch and his friends have assumed that God punishes the evildoer and rewards the good. But what if reality is the exact reverse. Job has already hinted at it, but in chapter 21 he develops it even more clearly. We can see this through the following outline.

Friend	Claim	Job's Reply
Zophar	Wicked die prematurely (20:11)	7, 13
Bildad	Wicked die childless (18:19)	8, 11
Eliphaz	If Job is righteous, his home will be safe (5:24)	9
All of them	Wicked do not prosper long (20:5)	17, 18

Eliphaz, Zophar	Children suffer for sins of parents (5:4; 20:10)	19-21
Bildad	Light of wicked extin- guished (18:5)	17
Zophar	God vents anger against wicked (20:23)	17-31

Employing example after example, Job shows what everyday experience teaches us: the wicked do not always receive their automatic punishment. They and their children often live prosperous lives and die honored and mourned deaths, while the good often suffer without reason. People simply do not receive what they deserve. And whether good or bad, everyone meets the same fate (verse 26). If you don't believe me, Job declares to his friends, just ask the ordinary man or woman on the street (verses 29, 30). As for the idea that the children of the wicked receive punishment for their parents, Job explodes, "Let it be paid back to them [the parents], so that they may know it" (verse 19). For God to do otherwise is unjust.

"How then will you comfort me with empty nothings?" the patriarch concludes. "There is nothing left of your answers but falsehood" (verse 34).

Chapter 22 begins the third cycle of speeches. Oddly, it is an incomplete cycle. Bildad has an unusually short speech, and Zophar none at all. Job now seems to support ideas and arguments that his friends had previously used against him (see, for example, Job 24:18-24; 26:5-14; 27:13-23). Scholars have offered all kinds of explanations, including that of a damaged text. Commentaries propose all kinds of rearrangements and reconstructions of the text to fill in the missing gaps of a third cycle.

We will not deal with this problem except to

observe that the book is a difficult one and that the debate between Job and his friends has clearly reached an impasse. The friends have run out of arguments, and what little communication once existed between them and Job has now ceased altogether.

In Job 22:2-4 Eliphaz repeats his previous claim that human beings are inherently worthless to God, but he quickly zeroes in on Job and his obvious—to Eliphaz, anyway—wickedness. His voice dripping with sarcasm, he demands, "Is it for your piety that he reproves you, and enters into judgment with you?" (verse 4).

After declaring that Job is a great sinner (verse 6), Eliphaz begins listing his crimes, first starting with the social realm—Job's moral faith (verses 6-11). Eliphaz charges that Job has failed his social and community responsibilities. (The patriarch will defend himself against these crimes in chapter 29). Old Testament religion emphasized righteousness, not as some abstract quality, but as how God's people treated each other and those around them. Helping one's neighbor was just as fundamental as avoiding carnal thoughts, offering sacrifices, or not stealing, lying, or committing murder. Righteousness was the whole way the believer lived. By saying that Job ignored the widow or orphan or did not care for the thirsty and hungry, Eliphaz meant that the patriarch was an unrighteous person, or sinner.

This Old Testament perspective carries over into the New Testament, as we see in Matthew 25:31-46. Here, one of the few places in the New Testament that tells exactly what God will judge His people about, Christ shows God judging His professed followers, not on what they believe (doctrine), but on how they treat others (discipleship).

Next Eliphaz turns to Job's alleged theological heresies (Job 22:12-20). He charges that the patriarch has said that because God is high in the heavens (verse 12), He does not know what the wicked are up to (verses 13, 14). However, Job has never claimed this, rather the exact opposite—God sees too much (Job 7:19, 20; 13:27; 14:3, 6; 16:9). Eliphaz reminds Job that God has punished those in the past who thought this same thing (Job 22:16) even if they did tell Him to get lost (verse 17). The verse echoes Job's quote of the wicked in Job 21:14, 15. In Job 22:17, 18 Eliphaz almost confirms Job's claim of chapter 21 that God bestows good on the wicked.

Eliphaz has first attacked Job's character, then his theological orthodoxy. His behavior reflects the eternal pattern of theological infighting. And Eliphaz has structured his accusation exactly like certain prophetic oracles to give it greater religious authority. [3] He is determined to beat down even further the suffering patriarch.

After savagely attacking Job, Eliphaz then tells him that if he repents and returns to God, he will be fully restored (verses 21-30). People who indulge in theological controversy too often cruelly assume that despite the fact they have wounded and mauled others in the name of God, their victims will still want to rush to God's arms even though they have acted as His fists. Eliphaz has many good and true things to say, but how can Job possibly hear them over the pain his friend has inflicted on him? Especially in light of Eliphaz' unrelenting conviction that Job is guilty (verse 30)?

Job's words in chapter 23 are not addressed either to his friends or to God, but are the anguished struggle of a devout believer who is overwhelmed by the fact that God remains silent no matter how hard he pleads for an answer. In verses 1-9 he has lost his sense of God's presence.[4] God has withdrawn into darkness in contrast to the "celestial harassment" he thought he felt in chapter 10. If only he knew where to find God (Job 23:3; cf. 8, 9), then he would argue his case before Him (verse 4) and find out God's position (verse 5). Strangely, Job expects to get a fair hearing (verses 6, 7), even though he has repeatedly complained about divine injustice.

Himself slipping back into the concept of retribution that he has been periodically struggling against, he believes that he would win his trial against God because he has been pure (verses 10-12). God has been testing him, and he will come through it all like refined gold (verse 10). But then he begins to waver, and fear floods back over him once more (verses 13-17). "If only I could vanish in darkness, and thick darkness would cover my face!" (verse 17). Hope and despair alternately wash over him. The pious Job of spiritual myth does not exist. This is the real Job—a Job who struggles and agonizes every inch of the way toward faith.

Chapter 24 is full of complex images, verbs with unspecified subjects, and pronouns with unclear antecedents. In the words of Edwin Good, "Translators have an inordinately hard time with it, changing singulars to plurals and finding conjecture necessary. . . . Any interpreter must confess uncertainty about this passage."[5]

Job echoes the later prophet Habakkuk, who also demanded to know why an all-powerful God permits suffering. The patriarch lists a series of crimes that indicate social disintegration. Because religious belief guided all Old Testament behavior, such violations also reflect religious collapse.

Verse 2: The wicked remove boundary stones between fields, confusing property lines. Without modern surveying techniques, it might take some time before the rightful landowner noticed the theft of cropland. Evildoers steal other flocks and mingle them with their own animals. In an economy without factories and service industries, land and herds were almost the only source of income, and to lose either would quickly lead to slavery or starvation and death.

Verse 3: Old Testament law defined both the orphan and widow by the fact that they had no family to help them survive. The donkey and the ox would be equivalent to the pickup truck and farm tractor of today. Such animals would help them to grow food or earn income. The loss of either would be fatal.

Verse 4: The wicked treat the poor with contempt instead of caring for their needs, as was the divinely ordained responsibility of the community.

Verse 5: The poor find themselves reduced to the state of animals forced to forage for anything they can find to eat.

Verse 6: Without land or herds of their own, the poor have to toil for the wicked, who either stole their capital property or defrauded them of it. To survive at all, the poor have to sell themselves into slavery.

Verses 7, 8, 10: Because clothing was expensive and difficult to make, the ancients often had only one or two changes of garments at a time. The cost of clothing was equivalent to what people in modern societies might pay for furniture, appliances, or even an automobile. Moneylenders would often take clothing as a pledge or security for a loan. The loss of any coat or outer garment would force the poor to endure the cold nights of Palestine without adequate protection. If a person did have to use his cloak as a pledge on a loan, biblical law required the moneylender to return it before nightfall.

Verse 9: The wicked demand helpless infants as security for loans.

Verses 10, 11: Job describes the poor reduced to servitude, reaping crops they were not allowed to share. In Leviticus 19:9, 10, God commanded His people to leave some of the crop unharvested for the poor and resident alien to gather for their survival. Here in Job the wicked leave no provision for their impoverished laborers.

Verse 12: Although the community had responsibility for caring for the dying and the wounded, the wicked shirk their duty. He implies that the wicked get away with so much simply because God pays no attention to what they do.

Verses 13-17: The patriarch lists a series of deeds done under cover of darkness. In the unlighted streets of the villages one could get away with all kinds of crimes, from murder to immorality. The thief could dig through the mudbrick or rubble and plaster walls of the average house without being seen.

Verses 18-20: The kinds of crimes Job has already described bring a curse on the land and the people.

Verses 21-24: God even prolongs the lives of those who do such deeds.

Verse 25: Finally, Job challenges anyone to prove his description of the wicked wrong. If we will just be honest and recognize what we constantly see, ordinary experience demonstrates the falsity of the doctrine of retribution.

Although Job has challenged his friends to prove him wrong, none of them ever respond to it, and strangely enough, God never criticizes him at the end of the book for such rash statements. The Deity understands the despair that drove His servant to make them, and, beyond that, experience confirms the truth-fulness of much of what he has said.

Commentator Edwin Good wonders why Job still wants a trial with the kind of God he has portrayed. Not only does Job believe that God hides from him, but that He is corrupt and corrupts everything around Him. In fact, Job finds the fingerprints of God on every evil deed. [6]

But the patriarch still wants that hearing before God. Does another part of himself sense that God is really not like that at all? What continues to fan that faint flicker of hope that despite everything refuses to let go of the Deity? Is it the memory of his previous experience with the Lord of the universe that has ignited his spark of hope and keeps it ready to burst into flame?

Bildad's reply in chapter 25 is only six verses long. Some commentators have suggested that the rest of his speech may continue in a later chapter, [7] while others feel that such attempts "are not convincing, if only because the number and variety of competing solutions leave the student quite dizzy." [8] Balmer H. Kelly offers as one possibility the idea that the author may have shortened the speech to symbolize the defeat of Job's friends in the debate. [9]

Regardless of the reason for the length of the speech, Bildad's low opinion of God's human creation is clear. It is not a new thought. Eliphaz first brought the attitude up in Job 4:17-21 and repeated it in Job 15:14-16 and Job 22:1-4. Zophar attacked the value of human beings in Job 11:5-12. The patriarch echoed such sentiments himself when he said that God had infinitely greater wisdom (Job 9:2-12; 12:9-25; and 14:4).

Psalm 14:1-4 and Romans 3:10 also speak of human depravity. But a recognition of the fallen condition of humanity does not explain why Job has experienced such unusual suffering. Does a person who has stolen or told a lie deserve to have his entire family killed by a drunken driver? Can even an evil person suffer unfairly?

Although Bildad may call a human being a "maggot" and a "worm" (Job 25:26) in God's sight, the rest of Scripture shows that God puts a far different value on His human creation (cf. Psalm 8). Romans 3:10 is speaking about man's inability to save himself. But otherwise he is of infinite worth.

Is Bildad projecting his own opinion of Job into the mind of God Himself? And is this still another sad result of theological controversy? That to defend our own beliefs, we must devalue the worth of those who may hold different views? Little does Bildad realize that as he condemns Job he also condemns himself.

---

[1] The Hebrew has a masculine singular "you" before "mock." Is he addressing Zophar, Eliphaz, who will speak next; or, as Edwin Good suggests ("Job," in *Harper's Bible Commentary*, p. 420), God Himself here? Verse 4, with its question "is my complaint addressed to mortals?" might suggest God. In the second cycle of speeches Job has become more and more hostile to God and has spoken to Him less and less. If the singular "you" is a direct address to God, it is the first one since chapter 19.

[2] Andersen, *Job: An Introduction and Commentary*, pp. 197, 198.

[3] Good, p. 421.

[4] Simundson, *The Message of Job*, p. 94.

[5] Good, p. 422.

[6] *Ibid.*

[7] For example, A. van Selms suggests that Job's reply in Job 26:1-14 could just as easily have been given by either Bildad or Zophar (*Job: A Practical Commentary*, p. 7).

[8] Andersen, p. 214.

[9] Kelly, *The Book of Ezra; The Book of Nehemiah; The Book of Esther; The Book of Job*, p. 113.

Where Is Wisdom?

10

WE HAVE already mentioned that the next few chapters have long puzzled commentators and scholars. Bildad's reply is strangely short, Zophar has no speech at all, and Job says things that seem to contradict his previous positions. But J. Gerald Janzen suggests that Job's apparent contradiction may represent something else.

Janzen points out that the patriarch often quotes snatches from the arguments of his friends, employing the phrases in a sarcastic or ironical manner. Some of the passages in Job's speeches that appear to contradict his previous arguments, Janzen believes, fall into this category. [1] These are hard to detect because ancient manuscripts did not have quotation marks or other punctuation, or even break the strings of letters into sentences and paragraphs. The Bible was originally meant to be read out loud by someone already familiar with the text.

The opening verses of chapter 26 drip with sarcasm as Job declares "How you have helped one who has no power!" and "How you have counseled one who has no wisdom, and given much good advice!" (verses 2, 3). Job uses the first person singular as he addresses Bildad, a form previously reserved only for God. Is the patriarch talking about himself or God? Could he be striking out at God through his human friend? Either way he dramatically portrays his friends' failure to comfort him.

Commentators have generally not dwelt on this failure as much as they should have. We may disagree with another's theology, but we still have the responsibility to care for him or her. Unlike Job's friends, we must not stand by and let someone suffer unaided, no matter who that person is or what he or she believes.

Verses 5-14 are a beautiful hymn to God's power in creation that some scholars have assigned to Bildad.[2] The ideas in the poem are general enough to have come from the lips of anyone in the book. Simundson suggests, though, that if Job was talking about God in verses 2 and 3, the passage would be Job's way of "emphasizing the power of God and highlighting the preposterous pretension of mortals who feel the need to come to the aid of a God like that."[3]

Another possibility might be that Job is using the poem to refute something Eliphaz said earlier. In Job 4:12-21 he claimed that a voice or spirit of inspiration gave him insight that showed where Job was wrong in his reasoning. Now in chapter 26 Job could be attempting to disprove Bildad with spiritual insight that he feels he has gained from nature, the source of inspiration especially admired in the wisdom tradition.

Job 26:12, 13 employs imagery that God will pick up in His great speech to Job. The poem concludes with the question "But the thunder of his power who can understand?" (verse 14). Apart from two or three exceptions, thunder in the Old Testament indicates God either revealing Himself to His people or delivering or saving them. The Deity will soon thunder from the whirlwind.

In chapter 24 Job has painted a dark picture of God. Yet in chapter 27 he declares his integrity through an oath on God's life (verses 2-6). It is the last resort of a man who feels that he has no choice left but to turn his case over to God Himself. Francis Andersen says that handing one's case over to God—the ultimate custodian of justice—through invoking a solemn oath was an approach of last resort and a way of staying a trial. Appealing to God as the impartial punisher of perjury might be an innocent man's only defense against false testimony or of resolving a case in which there was not enough evidence to lead to any kind of verdict. Job feels that he is trapped in both predicaments here. [4]

Simundson observes that even though Job accuses God of taking "away my right" and making "my soul bitter" (verse 2), he still utters his oath in the name of that same God. While Job believes that God must bear responsibility for what happened to him, yet he still fondly remembers the Lord as a loving Creator, a Deity that one can always approach in hope of obtaining justice, compassion, and vindication. [5] Even though God may terrify Job, the patriarch cannot relinquish his hold on Him. Something is tugging at his soul despite what he perceives as God's inherent evil. The divine Spirit reaches out to him and he responds, even though he has a host of unanswered and unanswerable questions. And that is what God longs for in every one of His followers.

Job may wonder if perhaps he has done something wrong, as his friends suggest; he does not understand what has been happening to him, but he refuses to abandon his sense of integrity (verses 5, 6). Yet his friends have hurt him, and in verses 7-23 he longs for them to meet what he considers their just fate. Such common behavior raises a number of moral and theological issues. Is it wrong to wish that the wicked, especially those who have hurt us, should receive punishment for what they have done? When does a desire for justice shade into mindless revenge? What questions would the redeemed struggle with throughout eternity if God did not balance this cosmic equation of sin and punishment? And how does all this explain why God must raise the wicked dead at the second resurrection of Revelation 20?

One of the ways that Job believes God should punish the wicked is to destroy their means of security. Verses 14-18 mention several things the ancients considered to be sources of such security. They included:

• Children (both to preserve the family line and to support one in old age).

• Silver (the ancients used metal bars for trade instead of coins; at one time the Egyptians considered silver more valuable than gold because Egypt has few if any silver deposits).

• Clothing (as already mentioned, clothing was valuable and scarce).

• Houses (people would inherit a quarter or a sixteenth of a room, so living space—let alone a whole house—was a highly prized possession).

Job declares that all these indications of prosperity and security that the wicked have accumulated to protect themselves would be swept away overnight as events brought them their just punishment. And it does happen—as events in Eastern Europe have so forcefully reminded us.

Chapter 28 appears to be an interlude in the book. It mentions no speaker by name, and commentators have offered many proposals for its author or source and its purpose. Tradition usually ascribes it to Job, though many have suggested one of the friends or even the author of the book himself.[6] Although the search for wisdom is a continual refrain throughout the book of Job, why the poem appears here and not elsewhere in the book is also unknown.

The poem compares the search for wisdom to the hunt for valuable metals and gemstones. Mining to the ancients was about as difficult as is space exploration to us today. The ancients did not have the sophisticated tools or techniques of today's mining technology, but even modern historians of science stand in awe at how ancient men with crude tools and sputtering torches and tiny oil lamps hewed through the ground to find veins of metal or deposits of prized minerals and gemstones. They dared the underground dangers of rockfall, poisonous gas, and crippling accident to mine the earth's treasures.

Sometimes just getting to the site of a mine was an adventure in itself. Mines were often in remote areas, such as those at Timnah and the Arabah near Edom, or the turquoise mines of Serabit el-Khadem. The ancient Egyptians were so proud of their mining expeditions into the forbidding desert of the Sinai and elsewhere that they recorded them on their tomb walls.

We often think of the world of the Bible as an agrarian and pastoral one, but here is praise to ancient technology. The Bible writers could appreciate whatever man turned his knowledge and skills to if it was not done for evil ends.

Edwin Good declares that "the ancient world understood wisdom, it seems, principally as skill,"[7] thus its comparison to the technological skills of mining and technology in this chapter.

The miner's work and goal were hidden from even the sharpest eye—here the keen-eyed bird of prey (verse 7)—as was wisdom and the path to it. Human beings do not know how to find wisdom (verse 13), nor can they put a value on it (verses 15-19).[8] Not even death will reveal wisdom (verses 21, 22). Only God knows where wisdom is (verse 23), because He established it (verse 27) and defined it: "Truly, the fear of the Lord, that is wisdom; and to depart from evil is understanding" (verse 28).

Elsewhere the Old Testament portrays wisdom as a person. The book of Proverbs personifies wisdom as a woman (see Prov. 1:20-33; 8; etc.). The imagery that the Hebrew Scriptures use to describe wisdom is in the New Testament applied to Jesus. The teaching of both Testaments is the same: to get wisdom is to get God, to have an intimate relationship with Him. Job once had this, and he desperately longs for it again.

Edwin Good comments that "the ancient Israelites would have found our research universities, laboratories, and government grants unthinkable. Wisdom for them arises from religion ('fear of the Lord' = religion) and from morality. To be wise is to be religious and to avoid evil. Where have we seen that remark before? We were told that Job 'feared God [or was religious] and avoided evil' back in Job 1:1. More than that, God Himself described Job in the same terms (1:8; 2:3). Job possesses what the poem presents as the divine definition of wisdom. This chapter adds to Job's powerful assertion of his moral righteousness (Job 27:4-6) the claim to divinely certified wisdom."[9]

The debates are over, and Job's three friends have nothing more to say. They have never spoken to each other; they have never questioned each other or discussed any kind of strategy or goal in their attempt to reach and to help the patriarch. Debaters never do listen to anyone except themselves. All they have done is once again show the utter inability of debate to change minds or help anyone.

The patriarch concludes this section of the book. In his speech he recounts his past life, agonizes over the condition he now finds himself in, and continues to struggle with his inexplicable suffering. He does not speak to or mention his three friends. Except for a few verses in chapter 30, where he speaks directly to God, chapters 29 to 31 are basically a soliloquy. Although he generally addresses the reader—or in the ancient world, the listener—it is really his final appeal to God to break His long silence and speak to him.

Job will summarize his case—his fall from blessing and privilege to mockery and anguish—in three parts:

1. A description of the "good old days" when he was prosperous and honored by his community (chapter 29).

2. A lament of his miserable present (chapter 30).

3. The use of a series of curses to clear himself of the accusations against himself (chapter 31).

Until the bandits and whirlwind swept out of the desert, Job had lived a happy and prosperous life, and like millions before and after, he had thought it would

116

never change. But sudden disaster wiped away everything. Now he looks back at his former life with an incredible ache. God's friendship had been close and intimate (Job 29:2-5), and he had the respect and honor of everyone, high or low (verses 7-11). Job had been the model citizen, helping the needy and fulfilling every worthy civic responsibility (verses 11-25). Each example he gives illustrates and amplifies the virtue alluded to in Job 1:1, 8, and 2:3. He was a living demonstration of Old Testament moral righteousness and justice (Job 29:14).

Job was no hypocrite—he was a true disciple of a loving God. The patriarch may be proud of his former life, [10] but he has honest and honorable reason to be. As God proclaimed to the heavenly assembly, Job was His servant, His representative of godliness. But then everything fell apart for Job, as it has in countless other lives.

Chapter 30 is Job's lament for his lost life.[11] Those who had once honored him now made sport of him (verses 1-15). He struggles with the humiliation that people whom he would have once considered outcasts now ridicule him through satirical songs or use him as a byword of everything contemptible (verse 9). Like a cloud on a hot desert day, his prosperity has vanished into thin air (verse 15).

Job is a real and complex human being. His behavior cannot be neatly labeled and classified. How can we reconcile his feelings of resentment with God's description of him as blameless? Does his opinion of the outcasts or rabble throw into question his claims of compassion for the poor and needy in chapter 29? Do his words demonstrate prejudice and class consciousness, or do they reveal grief and hurt? If the latter, when does grief and hurt become sin? Or are these questions best left to God alone to decide?

The patriarch lays the blame for everything that has happened on God Himself (Job 30:16-19). It has to be Him. Who else could it be? Night and day he suffers. Like an angry, short-tempered man, God grabs Job by his lapels and shakes him until his teeth rattle. When Job manages to catch his breath and sob out the question Why? God cruelly remains silent. The only sound he hears is that of the storm that killed his children still howling through his life (verse 22), tossing and whirling him toward death (verse 23).

Perhaps again thinking of his prosperous days, Job expresses bitter disappointment that his moral and upright life has brought him only heartache (verses 24-31). Sadly he was the victim of his religious beliefs, of the insidious distortion of the doctrine of retribution. Simundson explains that "Job had been careful to do what a good religious person is supposed to do. Surely God would reward him for his good deeds. He could expect to die after a peaceful old age, in his own place, with his children around him, full of vigor to the end. But it did not turn out that way. And Job, as many other religious people, felt betrayed, because he had done his part but God had not upheld God's end of the bargain. If one expects to be rewarded for pious deeds, the disillusionment can be overwhelming when the anticipated rewards are not forthcoming." [12] The patriarch believes that he has always been merciful to others, yet God has not been merciful to him.

In chapter 31 Job makes his final defense of his life. In it he repeats and expands on themes that have appeared through his previous speeches. At times it may seem arrogant and self-centered to our Christian perspective. We would feel uncomfortable making some of the statements he did. Our sense of the deceitfulness and impact of sin on the human personality makes us cautious about uttering such declarations. But to the ancients, this was a familiar way of expressing one's moral condition.

The ancient Egyptians believed that after death they would undergo a trial in the Judgment Halls of Osiris. As a part of the process of judgment they would recite a systematic denial of a wide range of sins and misdeeds. The Egyptians carved these denials—often called the Negative Confessions or Declaration of Innocence—on their tomb walls or wrote them on papyrus and put them in their coffins.

Job goes through a long list of sins such as deceit (verses 5, 6), adultery (verses 9-12), [13] failing to help the disadvantaged (verses 13-23), idolatry (verses 24-28), gloating over the misfortunes of others (verses 29, 30), or defrauding others of land or its bounty (verses 39-40). Every so often he gives a solemn oath that he has not done any of them and suggests what could have happened to him if he had. Many of the sins remind us of those in the Egyptian texts. [14] But unlike the Egyptian parallel, they do not include magical incantations or spells guaranteed to protect him.

The patriarch means to say through his list, "If I have done any of these things, may a curse come down upon me." The ancients took such curses extremely seriously, [15] and Job would never inflict such a thing upon himself if he had the slightest question that he might be guilty of any of the offenses (cf. Ps. 7:3-5; 18:20-26).

The list of sins he vows that he has not committed involves "the violation of concrete social relations."[16] The patriarch cites at least 13 or 14 examples of specific relationships either with fellow human beings or between humanity and God. He claims that he is righteous because he has been blameless in his relationships with others, fulfilling them as society and God expected them to be. His concern is not whether he broke some kind of abstract law or is tainted by some abstract quality known as sin, but that he lived the kind of life expected of a person who cares for and respects others. Put all together, his examples describe in concrete terms a man "blameless and upright, one who feared God and turned away from evil" (Job 1:1).

In Job 31:35-37[17] Job makes one final challenge to God. If only the Deity would write out His indictment against Job, the patriarch would proudly wear it like a crown and approach Him like a prince. He would put his signature on it. "Resolutely, Job places his *taw*, the last letter of the Hebrew alphabet, originally made in the form of an X, on his complaint. . . . Job fears no indictment. He is fully convinced of his innocence."[18]

The patriarch will not speak again until God answers. But one more friend is waiting in the wings, ready to seize center stage.

---

[1] Janzen, *Job*, pp. 172, 173. A similar phenomenon has confused the readers of at least one New Testament writer. The apostle Paul would cite the slogans of his opponents, then refute them. For example, in 1 Corinthians 6 he quotes such slogans as "All things are lawful for me" (verse 12) and "Food is meant for the stomach and the stomach for food" (verse 13), then proceeds to refute them with qualifiers, as the reader can see most clearly in modern translations such as the New Revised Standard Version, which puts the slogans in quotation marks.

WHERE IS WISDOM?

2 Notice that Job 27:1 states that "Job again took up his discourse," implying some kind of gap.

3 Simundson, *The Message of Job*, p. 99.

4 Andersen, *Job: An Introduction and Commentary*, p. 220.

5 Simundson, pp. 99, 100.

6 One conservative introduction to the Old Testament makes the following observation: "If this is a purposeful interlude, it should be credited to the final author, who uses it to bring one phase of the book to a close and prepare for the next. As though reflecting on the stalemate to which the windy dialogue has led, he muses on the human inability to discover, buy, or discern true wisdom without divine help. Indeed, that is his summary of the book this far: neither Job nor the friends have found the key. By pointing to the need for divine help . . . he sparks anticipation for the speeches from the whirlwind (chapter 38)" (La Sor, *Old Testament Survey*, p. 566).

7 Good, "Job," in *Harper's Bible Commentary*, p. 424.

8 Verse 17 mentions glass in the same breath as gold as something valuable. When the ancients first began to work with glass, it was so difficult to make and thus valuable that Egyptians and others used pieces of glass in royal jewelry.

9 Good, p. 424.

10 Commentators have worried that there is a hint of self-satisfied arrogance here. Could Job be acceptable in God's sight, yet still harbor a touch of the overbearing?

11 Many assume that Job was an old man, but others believe that he was at the height of his vigor when the tragedies struck him. The Hebrew of Job 29:4 that is often translated "autumn days" literally means "in the days of fruit gathering," that is, the most productive period of life. Thus the NRSV translates it "when I was in my prime."

12 Simundson, p. 114.

13 Verses 9 and 10 contain a strange curse in which the consequence of any infidelity he might have committed would fall upon his wife. Could there be a lingering hurt from when his wife had urged him to curse God?

14 For example, chapter 125 of the Egyptian Book of the Dead.

15 "We must remember . . . that these are actually *curses* that Job calls down on himself. The curse in the ancient world was no casual expression but was the most powerful way one had to set in motion forces of action and reaction. The curse worked itself out, objectively and irresistibly, and even God could not hinder it. Our culture has nothing that corresponds to it, and we tend not to understand why other cultures have taken curses so seriously. . . . Job lays his own future and welfare on the line. If he is mistaken about anything in his claims to moral integrity, the unspoken catastrophe will strike him still further down" (Good, p. 427).

16 Janzen, p. 213.

17 One would expect this passage to come at the end of the curses. Scholars have no explanation for its position.

18 Gladson, *Who Said Life Is Fair?* p. 81.

Job's Final Test

──────────── **11** ────────────

JOB has ended his defense and the three friends have run out of arguments. It would seem that it was now time for God to present His side of the argument. But the climax will be postponed as a new individual enters the discussion. Elihu listened to at least part of the dialogues, and as he did so he became more and more frustrated. Scripture says he was angry—angry at Job for trying to justify himself rather than upholding God, and angry at the three friends for failing to answer Job's arguments (Job 32:2, 3, 5). [1] Also, as Norman C. Habel observes, his ego matches his anger. [2]

The Elihu speeches have puzzled readers for centuries because they seem anticlimactic and even unnecessary. Some have even suggested that they were stuck into the book by a later editor. They have differences in style and vocabulary from the rest of the book. But others feel that they play an important role in the development of its themes. Scholars offer a number of possible reasons for his speeches:

1. Elihu gives a different answer to Job's problem than the others have. His speeches show how suffering can be revelatory, emphasize the stern nature of God's love, and hint at a kind of righteousness by faith.

2. He offers a correct but uncomfortable answer (for example, that Job is guilty and responsible for his fate),

thus relieving God of the responsibility of having to say it (a popular Jewish view of Elihu from the Middle Ages onward).

In a similar vein, Norman C. Habel suggests that Elihu's speeches give a seemingly plausible and orthodox resolution of Job's problems, one that many religious believers would accept. However, it is a false solution, as God's speeches will reveal, because it deals with the problem only from a human perspective and experience. [3] Elihu, as does every other human being in the book, finds himself trapped in partial truth. Partial truth leads to distorted conclusions.

3. His speeches have been suggested as a means of preparing Job for God's speeches. The patriarch had tuned out his first three friends, but might have been more receptive to someone else repeating the same ideas. It is a common human experience to ignore what one person tells us but to listen to another, even though he or she is saying the same thing. We respond to some people better than others.

4. The speeches maintain dramatic tension by delaying the appearance of the divine voice. [4]

5. David Noel Freedman sees the Elihu speeches as the Satan's fourth test of Job's character, his final attack on the patriarch. [5]

The name Elihu means "my God is he" or "he is God," [6] but he will be anything except divine in what he hurls at Job. He says that he did not speak before because he wanted to defer to his elders (verses 4, 6, 7), but he comes across simply as brash and pretentious as he disparages the other three friends (verses 11-15). Rejecting the idea that age brings wisdom, he claims that his came from the divine spirit or "breath" in him, the same spirit that God breathed into man in the Creation story (verse 8; cf. Job 33:4 and Ex. 35:30, 31). Elihu fears that he is about to "burst" from the activity of God's Spirit (verses 18-20). [7]

God does reveal truth through the Holy Spirit. So far Elihu is correct. But what he has to say about Job and the cause of his suffering dramatically indicates that the Holy Spirit is really not speaking to him. He wants to defend God, but like too many who have claimed to have an inner access to truth, God is not with him.

After vowing that he will be impartial and flatter no one (verses 21, 22), he tediously launches his onslaught against Job and soon demonstrates that he regards himself as totally on God's side. In fact, he believes that he has to defeat Job at any cost to uphold God.

Chapters 33-37 divide his wordy monologue (the patriarch never answers him) into four speeches by the phrase "Elihu continued and said" (Job 34:1; 35:1; and 36:1). [8] In Job 33:4 he appears to be claiming a special authority, a common temptation in religious controversy. However, he quickly downplays it by claiming that he and Job are on an equal footing through creation (verse 6). He alternates between superiority and "I'm just like you," both devices that can quickly become manipulative.

Although assuring Job that he would deal gently with him (verse 7), [9] Elihu treats the patriarch much as the other three friends have. He recounts Job's defense of himself and tells Job that he was wrong to claim innocence (verses 8-12). Why? Because "God is greater than any mortal" (verse 12). Elihu instantly disproves his claim of impartiality. He is on what he believes is God's side, and thus totally opposed to Job. As with so many caught up in theological controversy, the claim to be on God's side leads him to assume that he is automatically right and everyone else is wrong.

After asking how Job can possibly say that God won't speak to him, Elihu spends most of the rest of chapter 33 describing how God does communicate to man through two important channels. First, God may speak through dreams and night visions (verse 15). Such dreams and visions seek to warn and terrify human beings so that they will change their ways and escape disaster and destruction (verses 16-18). Second, God uses pain and suffering itself—especially illness—as a way of correcting His followers (verse 19).

However, as in the case of Job, one may misinterpret the meaning and significance of such illness. Elihu then describes individuals who have become so sick that they have reached the point of death (verse 22). God then sends an angel or mediator to one of them. The angelic mediator speaks to God on the person's behalf (verses 24-26), and the man turns to God, who accepts and saves him (verse 26). In gratitude the person praises God before others, telling everybody that though he had deserved death as a sinner, God waived that punishment (verses 27, 28). Clearly Elihu is hinting that Job should follow his illustration's example. (And does Elihu think that he is God's messenger to Job?)

Elihu, building on an earlier claim by Eliphaz (Job 5:17), sees suffering as something that God uses to refine and discipline. It is an idea championed by millions of other religious people. God can employ suffering as a teaching device, just as one can take a revolver and use it to pound nails, crush nuts, or keep papers from blowing off a desk though they are not the weapon's real purpose. But God did not create suffering as a divine teaching aid.

The brash young friend is also wrong because Job did not need any instruction or disciplining. God had told the Satan that Job was blameless and upright, hardly a description of someone requiring a good dose of suffering as further instruction. Job may learn something from his experience, but God did not inflict incomprehensible suffering on him for that reason.

After again telling Job to speak up if he has anything to say but to otherwise listen to him (verses 31-33), in chapter 34 Elihu defends God's justice. The second speech appears aimed either to the three friends or to the world at large, though he does address Job at the end (verse 35). It is the only time Elihu uses the patriarch's name.

Simundson describes Elihu as like those politicians who lift phrases from their opponents' speeches and then use the out-of-context quotes against them. [10] He twists Job's defense of himself into the polemic of a religious scoffer and then accuses him of consorting with evildoers and the wicked (verses 5-9). Elihu is trying to prove, among other things, Job's guilt by association with wicked individuals who have also employed such arguments. But the only ones who have visited Job recently have been him, Eliphaz, Bildad, and Zophar.

Elihu declares in verse 4, "Let us choose what is right; let us determine among ourselves what is good." The young man believes that unaided human reason will aid him and all other "wise men" (verse 2) in knowing what is good and bad. To a certain extent what he says is true. The conscience in tune with the Holy Spirit can determine whether much is right or wrong, as we see illustrated in the fact that all cultures and peoples have a sense of right and wrong. Even those who may not believe in God usually have an intuitive sense of morality and ethics. But Elihu's total misinterpretation of Job's situation shows the limitations of human reason unaided by special revelation.

Like Eliphaz in Job 22:17, Elihu plays into the Satan's hands with his claim that Job says there is no reward in serving God. The Satan had claimed in the prologue that Job served God only because of the hope of such reward.

Presenting about as clear a statement of the doctrine of retribution as there is in the whole book (Job 34:11), Elihu argues that God is the all-powerful sustainer of life (verses 13-15), thus whatever He does has to be by definition right and just. The brash young friend operates on the assumption that if you've got the power to rule, you will automatically rule justly and confront the wicked (verses 17-20).

In verses 21-30 he goes into detail on how God watches the wicked and deals with them in the presence of their fellow human beings. They cannot hide from Him (verses 21, 22). Whether they be individuals or whole nations, the godless shall not triumph (verse 30). We might not understand what He is doing, but we can be sure that He is just (verse 29). The Hebrew of verses 29-35 is uncertain, but in the rest of the chapter Elihu claims that any wise person who objectively looks at the facts will have to conclude that Job does not know what he is talking about (verses 34, 35) and that he sounds suspiciously like a sinner (verse 36). In fact, he is guilty of rebellion against God (verse 37). The more Job talks, according to Elihu, the greater his rebellion grows.

Elihu begins his third speech by claiming that Job said that he was in the right in his trial before God (Job 35:2). Actually the patriarch said—if anything—the exact opposite (cf. Job 9:2, 3). Few people involved in religious controversy can resist the temptation to put words into the mouth of an opponent. Also, Elihu explores the issue of whether anything that human beings do can affect God in any way (verses 5-7). While Job's wickedness or righteousness might have an impact on other human beings (verse 8), God exists above the mundane existence of the human race. For all his vaunted wisdom, Elihu only winds up going over issues and arguments that the other three friends had already worn out.

Next, Elihu attempts to deal with the issue Job has raised about God's silence and failure to respond to humanity's cries for help. In chapter 33 he stated that God does answer through dreams, suffering, and angels. Now he suggests that God may not answer because people did not really address their cries to Him (Job 35:9-11). Like the child who will not respond unless the family uses the name he has chosen for himself, God will not answer unless we speak to Him directly.

In verse 12 Elihu suggests that God ignores human beings because of their evil pride. And in verse 13 he states that God ignores an "empty" cry, apparently a general complaint about one's predicament in life and thus an indication of a person's wickedness. But people in pain often find it difficult to speak to God.

Suffering may have jolted their faith in Him or even raised doubts about His existence. Even though they desperately need His help, they are not sure whether they even want to talk to Him. Elihu has God setting up a kind of sincerity test to screen out requests for help that do not meet a certain divine standard.

Job claims that he has a case against God and is only waiting for God to respond to it (verse 14), but Elihu considers this arrogance on the patriarch's part. In fact, if God did answer, Job might not be so bold in his complaint against God (verses 15, 16).

Chapters 36 and 37 contain Elihu's fourth and last speech. Bragging on himself (Job 36:4), he declares that he will speak on God's behalf (verse 2) and extol God's righteousness (verse 3). In verses 5-7 he stresses how powerful and impartial God is—as if repeating something often enough will force another to believe against his or her will and experience. Then in verses 8-23 he expands on the theme that God instructs people through suffering. But his arguments totally ignore everyday human experience. How much do we really learn when we are in pain? Will a toothache make a student learn history or literature or biology better? If death snatches a loved one away, will the survivor appreciate God's love more? Yes, we can learn from pain, but it never guarantees that we will learn *better* or learn the *right thing*.

Elihu lectures Job for being "obsessed with the case of the wicked" (verse 17). But so is he and the other three friends. Not knowing how to relate Job's experience with their theological understanding, they judge him guilty and wicked and labor mightily to convince him of this fact. God is a great teacher, Elihu argues;

listen to Him (verse 22). But few human educational systems would tolerate the cruel methods he ascribes to God.

For the rest of his final speech (Job 36:26-37:24) Elihu extols God's majesty through a beautiful poem filled with nature imagery. Much of that imagery involves weather phenomena, showing how important water was in Palestine. Unlike the civilizations in Egypt and Mesopotamia that had great rivers for irrigation, the people of Palestine were totally dependent on rainfall for survival. Some years drought devastates the land, while other years heavy rain and even heavy snowfall (witness the floods, blizzards, and four-foot snowfalls of the 1991-1992 rainy season) bring abundant moisture to the land.

Reflecting the area's concern for precipitation, Baal, the major god of Canaan, was lord of the rain storms and rider of the clouds. Elihu here depicts the true God as ruler of the storm and custodian of the clouds, snow, and frost. Even in Israel a storm was a powerful manifestation of God's presence, as we see in Habakkuk 3:6 and elsewhere. Often in Scripture the storm represents God as a warrior exhibiting His wrath either for or against His people. Habakkuk 3:7-16 depicts the Lord going forth in the metaphor of a storm to "trample" the nations that had attacked God's people. In Judges 4 and 5 God delivers His people from King Jabin through a storm, and in 1 Samuel 7 He routed the Philistines with a sudden storm.

In Job 37:14-18 Elihu asks a series of questions that anticipate God's speech, which begins in chapter 38, but here they have a quite different motivation than when God raises them. The brash young human being is attempting to stop Job's protest against God by trying to show that the patriarch is so insignificant before the awesomeness of the Lord that he has absolutely no right to question the Deity. If Elihu can silence Job's questions, then perhaps the other theological issues the suffering patriarch is frightening them with will also go away.

Verse 18 appears to depict the clearing after the storm, using an image—that of the sky like a bronze mirror—that scholars have traced all the way back to ancient Sumer. But a storm still rages in Job's soul. And it will take the whirlwind of God to blow it away.

Elihu concludes his speech by reminding Job one last time of God's majesty, power, and justice (verses 22, 23). The Lord has a righteousness that He will never violate. "Therefore mortals fear him; he does not regard any who are wise in their own conceit" (verse 24). The young friend has forgotten his own claim that *he* had exalted wisdom. Though he thinks he judges Job, he is really the one that stands convicted by his own words.

---

[1] Four times Scripture says that Elihu's anger flared up.

[2] Habel, *The Book of Job*, p. 443.

[3] *Ibid.*, pp. 36, 37.

[4] A similar suggestion has been offered for why the book of Esther contains two banquet scenes instead of one.

[5] Freedman,"Is It Possible to Understand the Book of Job?" *Bible Review*, April 1988, p. 29. "He [Elihu] is the person assumed or adopted by Satan to press his case for the last time" (*ibid.*). This idea was first presented in the Testament of Job, a pseudepigraphic work dating from the time of the Romans (*ibid.*, p. 44).

[6] Elihu is the only friend with an Israelite name (Habel, p. 448).

[7] In Job 15:2 Eliphaz had asked, "Should the wise answer with windy knowledge, and fill themselves with the east wind?" Habel comments that the author has Elihu describe himself almost exactly in these words in Job 32:17-22 (*ibid.*, p. 444).

[8] Some take Job 36:26-37:22 as a fifth speech, even though it lacks the usual introduction.

[9] Though he does add, "Answer me, if you can" (verse 5). However, Job never does respond. Perhaps Elihu never gave him a chance.

[10] Simundson, *The Message of Job*, p. 128.

The Whirlwind

12

JOB had begged and pleaded for God to speak to him. Now the Deity does—out of the whirlwind, symbol both of the death of Job's children and the theophany of the Divine Presence. [1] Elihu had spoken of trembling before the thunder or presence of God. Job will do exactly that. And the awesome theophany would confirm Job's prediction in Job 9:3, 19 of what would happen when he did meet the Lord.

God will neither explain His case against Job nor give any reason for the disasters and suffering that had devastated the patriarch. Instead, He will overwhelm him with a series of questions whose only answers can be "I don't know" or "I can't." The questions will form two speeches, perhaps following an ancient stylistic pattern that the most important speaker in a discussion should speak twice. [2] Also, it could be paralleling the two stages of Job's suffering caused by the Satan's two-phased attack.

(Ancient Israelite literature was particularly concerned with symmetry and balance, perhaps as an aid to memorization.) Or it could indicate that for the first time in the poetic section genuine dialogue is now going on. Unlike the case with the friends, Job really listens to what God has been saying, and he responds to it. [3]

God's questions remind the reader of ones that his friends and even Job himself have previously raised. But God has a different purpose with His questions than the little group around the dustheap had in mind. Norman C. Habel outlines the plan of God's first speech in a table that compares God's questions with the parallel or related claim or question that Job had already made and shows their different intent or purposes. [4]

God's questions relate to His creative activities and follow the pattern of Creation outlined in Genesis 1, including references to the alternation of darkness and light and to the living beings in each sphere of creation. Strangely, however, He does not mention human beings as a part of creation. Perhaps He implies humanity in two of the types of questions that He employs. We could classify the questions as either "Who are you?" or "Where were you?" (The third type of question God uses in His speech is "Can you?")

God's speeches have troubled many commentators because they feel He comes across as a tyrant. A superficial reading may give the impression that God only wants to put Job in his place. But a more careful examination will reveal that God has no desire to humiliate Job or ridicule him.

Throughout this book Job and his four fellow human beings have argued as though they understood how the world operated. Despite the mystery of his suffering, even Job thought he had God all figured out. The patriarch never really rejected the principle of retribution—he just didn't understand how his case fit into it. Now through His questions God begins to open His servant's eyes to the fact that the world is far more complex than he had realized. The human beings in the book of Job have often spoken of God's power—now Job begins to realize the extent and awesomeness of that divine power.

God commences His first speech with the question "Who is this that darkens counsel by words without knowledge?" (Job 38:2). Although the speech is addressed at Job, it is not clear who exactly God has in mind here. Job? Elihu? All the friends? But it does not really matter. The divine questions challenge all humanity.

As already pointed out, the order of the questions follows that of Creation week. Habel outlines those in chapters 38 and 39 by specific domain.

The physical world
> The earth (Job 38:4-7)
> The sea (verses 8-11)
> The dawn (verses 12-15)
> The netherworld (verses 16-18)
> Light and darkness (verses 19-21)
> Weather phenomena (verses 22-30)
> Constellations (verses 31-33)
> Thunderstorm (verses 34-38)

The animal and bird kingdoms
> The lioness and the raven (Job 38:39-41)
> The ibex, or mountain goat, and fallow deer (Job 39:1-4)
> The wild ass (verses 5-8)
> The wild ox, or aurochs (verses 9-12)
> The ostrich (verses 13-18)
> The horse (verses 19-25)
> The hawk and the eagle, or vulture (verses 26-30) [5]

Through His questions God emphasizes that He alone has power to create. He shows how He has placed limits on the chaotic forces that could threaten His creation, something only He can do. For example, He has set boundaries for the sea (an ancient Near Eastern symbol for chaos), telling it, "Thus far shall you come, and no farther, and here shall your proud waves be stopped" (Job 38:11).

But even in His descriptions of how He controls the powerful forces of nature, God relates them to the human situation. For example, in His poetic imagery of dawn (verses 12-15) He reminds Job that while the wicked may do their thing in the darkness, when dawn and its light comes, it reveals and thus stops their evil deeds. Both the sea and the wicked can only go so far. Sin and suffering cause great tragedy, but they never destroy everything. We do not know why God draws the boundaries where He does, but we can trust that He knows what He is doing and seeks only His creation's ultimate good.

God may give freedom, but it is a limited freedom. The Deity does not explain why He permits evil and suffering, but He does declare that it has definite limits. Just as God addressed the sea in verse 11 and defined its limits, so He told the Satan that he could go only so far in his attacks on Job.

After exploring His creation of the earth and its physical phenomena, the Lord turns to His animate creation. Except for the horse (and it is an almost uncontrollable war horse), all the animals He lists are wild creatures from the deserts and rocky hills of Palestine.

God emphasizes that these creatures live independently of man. Even the war horse has an untamed aura about it as it responds to the excitement of the battle charge and can easily break from its driver's control (though Job 39:18 mentions a rider, men did not normally mount them yet—instead, the animals pulled chariots). The wild ox, or aurochs (not the unicorn of the KJV), was the most powerful of the hoofed animals. Only the hippopotamus and the elephant were larger land mammals. It became extinct in 1627.

The description of the ostrich is given from the perspective of the scientifically untrained observer. People in the ancient world considered it to be a silly bird. Whether or not the bird leaves its eggs to be trampled in the desert is beside the point. The animal was fearless and uncontrollable. It could laugh at the horse (verse 18), an image some commentators see as depicting the ostrich chasing the horse instead of the horse racing before it.

All these creatures are under God's care and protection. God is the one who has let the wild ass go free (verse 5), and He gives it the steppe and salt flat for its home (verse 6). He has made the ostrich forget wisdom (verse 17). The Lord endows the horse with strength and clothes it with its mane (verse 19). The hawk soars through the sky with the aid of the wisdom the Creator has provided, and the eagle or vulture makes its nest on lofty crags at divine command (verses 26, 27). The emphasis is not on "Why suffering?" but "Behold how He cares for His creation!" In essence God is saying to Job, "If I take pride in the horse and the lesser creatures of My creation, don't you think I care for you, one of the beings I made to rule over My creation? Yes, there are chaotic forces at loose in the world, but I put limits on them, just as I do the sea."

A child who has burned its hand on a hot pot or pan does not want explanations of cause and effect, or lectures on how pain protects us from accident or teaches us important lessons. The little one wants comforting and reassurance that everything will again be all right despite the pain. God could have explained the cosmic struggle going on behind the scenes over His servant Job, but He knew that the patriarch needed reassurance that God was capable of taking care of things more than he required explanations of the conflict between good and evil. Although God asked Job if he understood how the Deity operated in nature, the emphasis is not on scientific knowledge but God's concern and care for His creation.

God concludes His first speech by echoing the question He began it with. "Shall a faultfinder contend with the Almighty? Anyone who argues with God must respond" (Job 40:2; cf. Job 38:2, 3). God appears to be asking if Job wants to continue the argument any further. Speak up, He seems to say, or hold your peace.

J. Gerald Janzen compares God's question here to the one He raises in Jeremiah 12:5, where God expresses surprise over how quickly Jeremiah has succumbed to discouragement. "If you have raced with foot-runners and they have wearied you, how will you compete with horses?" The Lord wants to challenge the prophet "to a deeper loyalty and vocational endurance." Janzen believes that God is responding to Job in a similar way.[6] If you can't answer these "simple" questions, God implies, how do you expect to understand the issue of suffering? God does not accuse Job of moral faults, but does imply that he was in danger of theological insolence.

The Voice from the whirlwind has overwhelmed the patriarch. Along with Job 42:1-6, Job has never been at such a loss for words. Whether he has submitted to God or has just decided that it is more prudent not to say anything for the moment, we can only speculate. In Job 40:4 he tells God, "See, I am of small account; what shall I answer you? I lay my hand on my mouth."

Job's response means more than simply that God is powerful. In ancient Israelite justice those who acted as judge in a case were responsible for seeing that the decision was actually carried out. They had to implement the resulting justice. Job has been wanting to judge God, but he simply does not have the power or moral authority to put into effect any verdict against the Deity.

The Lord now addresses Job a final time. "Will you even put me in the wrong?" He asks. "Will you condemn me that you may be justified?" (verse 8). Job's friends have been defending God by arguing that the patriarch had to be guilty to deserve his suffering, while Job countered by claiming that God was guilty of all that had happened to him. All have been reasoning that suffering was an automatic sign of guilt. Job has been doing to God what his friends have been doing to him. Throughout the book their false premise has led them to argue the wrong questions and premises. Some have seen this as the central theme of the whole book: self-righteousness drives human beings to condemn God.

In verses 9-14 God tells Job that if He is guilty as charged, then let him, Job, take over and see if he can untangle the knots of human injustice and immorality. Let him deal with the proud and the wicked (verses 11-13). Thus God reminds Job that he does not have the power or ability to vindicate himself.

The Lord has raised the issue of divine power not to humiliate His servant or force him to acknowledge that he can't win any contest with Him. The Deity had a different purpose for His illustrations from nature. "Job must now realize that he is no more able to exercise jurisdiction in the moral realm than he is able to control the natural." [7]

To reinforce His point, God points to the mysterious Behemoth and Leviathan. Commentators have long debated over their identity. Some see them as exaggerated descriptions of real animals such as the hippopotamus and the crocodile. Others regard them as allusions to imaginary creatures well known by many cultures in the ancient Near East. Today, for example, we might speak of a ferocious person as a dragon, even though we realize that such creatures do not actually exist. Scripture often employs the image of Leviathan, as we see in Psalm 74:12-14; 104:25-28; and Isaiah 26:20-27:13, and perhaps echoes of the creature that appears in Revelation 12 and 13.

The important point here is not whatever they were in reality, but that "both creatures stand over against humankind as deadly, invincible, and enigmatic." [8] Scripture employs them as symbols of massive evil. God describes two creatures so awesome and powerful that it is obvious that Job can in no way control them. But the Lord can.

God follows a definite sequence in chapters 40 and 41. According to Edwin Good, God begins with "first the realm of humans (Job 40:9-14), then the realm of natural power beyond human force (Behemoth, verses 15-24), and finally the realm of supernatural, mythic power above creation (Leviathan, Job 41:1-34). The implication is clear: if Job wants to control the Deity by the power of his moral innocence, he must contend with forces that, though less than the Deity, are more than Job can handle."[9]

Only God can approach Behemoth with a sword (Job 40:19) or play with Leviathan as He would some monstrous pet, letting it sit on His hand or taking it for a walk on a leash (Job 41:5). They are dangerous beasts with much God-given freedom and autonomy. If Job can handle these things, then—and only then—could he possibly challenge God on the issue of cosmic justice.

The Lord has ended His speech to Job. The patriarch will respond briefly, and God will reprimand Job's friends, but God's servant will receive no further explanation of what happened to him. A fundamental part of Job's test was that he must struggle with the suffering without knowing its reason. If he knew the source of the attacks on him, the Satan would argue that the patriarch continued to cling to God because of expected reward from the One who would win the challenge. Thus God could not give concrete answers. Only evidence—and inconclusive evidence at that. Evidence that must be accepted and understood by faith. The rules of the test would not allow more than that.

Although God never tells Job why suffering runs amok in the world, He assures him that as He can control Behemoth and Leviathan, so He can subdue even the worst evil. He has shown Job that He cares for him, is aware of the human situation, and can intervene when in His wisdom He sees a compelling reason for doing so.

Despite the extensive and involved theological dialogues between Job and his friends, and God's speeches to Job, we have really learned almost nothing about the origin and meaning of suffering. We have seen only how Job and his friends related to his particular suffering. The book has given us no real reason that the Satan wanted to attack God's servant, or spelled out in any detail why God thought He must let it happen. God clearly saw a need for the assembled sons of God to witness the Satan's testing of Job, but the author never explains it.

David Noel Freedman believes that God bound Himself by certain terms in the testing of Job that limited any possible explanations. "Just as Satan may not finally kill Job, so God is not allowed to reassure Job about His positive and supportive interest in this frail human being. That would completely spoil the test." [10] Does this limitation also apply to how much the Deity can reveal to the watching heavenly assembly and also the reader of the book of Job itself? That the biblical reader must either figure things out for himself or await further revelation because this test involves not just Job but all creation?

A superficial reading of the prologue might make us think that Satan is the source of all suffering and tragedy, but the book has indicated that reality is far more complex than simply "the devil did it." Yes, the Satan did afflict Job, but the book has ignored him after the prologue, as though he were to a large extent irrelevant to the fundamental issue. The friends argued that suffering was either punishment or educational in nature, but by the way everyone's arguments eventually canceled each other out, the speeches revealed these approaches to be incomplete even at best.

What other factors, then, cause suffering? Do they explain its existence better, give it more reason and meaning? Or can suffering be explained at all? We will consider only two aspects.

The book of Job is full of creation imagery. The wisdom tradition was fascinated with God's creation. But the one aspect most wisdom writers overlooked was that God gave His creation great freedom. It mingles both order and unpredictability, a fact that modern science is only now beginning to appreciate in its studies of chaos in mathematics and the natural world.

Although the Old Testament generally views everything that happens as God's direct will, it also recognizes that humanity can rebel against God, and in fact has done so since its beginning. People can choose to obey or reject His will. Scripture is full of stories of human rebellion and of God's pleas for His people to return to Him. Joshua sums up God's constant call to humanity when he declares, "Choose this day whom you will serve" (Joshua 24:15).

God has given human beings the ability to choose, and the opportunity to make choices means that one can also make wrong choices—choices that either intentionally or unintentionally bring suffering to others. A nurse, for example, can administer the wrong medicine through inattention from exhaustion, confusion, distraction, or even a deliberate desire to kill.

But intelligent beings are not the only part of God's creation to have freedom. Experience teaches that even inanimate matter can have a limited amount. The book of Ecclesiastes, another book within the wisdom tradition and that also wrestles with the dark questions and deep issues of life, observed that "the race is not to the swift, nor the battle to the strong, nor bread to the wise, nor riches to the intelligent, nor favor to the skillful; but time and chance happen to them all" (Eccl. 9:11). "Time and chance"—unpredictability, randomness. Things can happen that are neither God's will, the Satan's, or anyone else's. They are simply the outworking of that limited freedom God bestowed on His creation.

A piece of structural steel does not cool properly at the foundry, producing a weak or stress point in the metal. One day it fractures, causing a bridge to collapse and killing and injuring the people who happen to be crossing at that moment. A gene fails to duplicate itself properly and triggers disease or mental retardation, perhaps passing itself on for generations. God constantly upholds His creation, but at the same time He allows it a limited but very real freedom of chance and circumstance, freedom that may sometimes lead to tragedy and suffering.

Jesus hints at this in His comment about the 18 people who died when a tower at the Pool of Siloam collapsed and fell on them (Luke 13:1-5). Although His point here is repentance, He implicitly acknowledges that accidents can happen without moral reason. Whether the tower was of flawed or shoddy construction or design or had weak stones in it does not matter here. Accidents occur, and when they do, we must not instantly make moral judgments about who deserved them.

But disturbing as this may be, it is the suffering that results from conscious decision that should really bother us. The book of Job cannot answer the unanswerable question of why people do such terrible things. It can only remind us that even the Leviathan of evil is under God's ultimate control. And chapter 42 will deliberately end on a happier note to remind us that God does have the power to say to suffering and tragedy, "Thus far and no farther."

[1] God appears in a whirlwind or storm in Psalm 18:7-15; 50:3; Ezekiel 1:4; Nahum 1:3; Habakkuk 3; and Zechariah 9:14.

[2] Selms, *Job: A Practical Commentary*, pp. 8, 9.

[3] Freedman, "Is It Possible to Understand the Book of Job?" *Bible Review*, April 1988, p. 30.

[4] Habel, *The Book of Job*, pp. 530-532.

[5] *Ibid.*

[6] Janzen, *Job*, p. 242.

[7] Andersen, *Job: An Introduction and Commentary*, p. 287.

[8] Gladson, *Who Said Life Is Fair?*, p. 96.

[9] Good, "Job," in *Harper's Bible Commentary*. p. 431.

[10] Freedman, p. 30.

"Now I See"

13

GOD has finished His second speech, and Job responds. The patriarch has received no answers to his questions, but he has learned that God is not elusive, that He is always present, even in suffering. The Lord knew that what Job really needed was not answers or explanations, but comfort. Just as children really need comfort and assurance instead of explanations when they hurt themselves, so do hurting adults. And the Voice from the whirlwind gave Job that comforting sense of the Divine Presence.

The whirlwind that God spoke from is an interesting image. A whirlwind can flatten houses and uproot trees, or it can bring the rain that all life depends on. The whirlwind symbolizes both the destruction that swept away the patriarch's children, and the awesome presence of God Himself, who gave Job those children in the first place. A strange contradiction, it reflects the way Scripture often reveals God, mingling seemingly contradictory truths. Revelation presents a God who is both love and wrath, who creates and destroys, who gives freedom yet is responsible for all that is, and who is always present while being forever beyond our grasp and understanding.

Job and his friends had often spoken about God's power. It had been a theoretical discussion, however.

But it is no longer theoretical to the patriarch. He has experienced it himself (Job 42:2). Repeating the question God had asked at the beginning of His first speech (Job 38:2), Job answers, "Therefore I have uttered what I did not understand, things too wonderful for me, which I did not know" (Job 42:3). To God's challenge, "I will question you, and you declare to me" (Job 42:4; cf. 38:3), God's servant responds, "I had heard of you by the hearing of the ear, but now my eye sees you" (Job 42:5). His encounter with God had changed him, and "his awareness of God cast a different perspective on suffering, making it not so much irrelevant as secondary to his knowledge of God." [1]

The patriarch has experienced God in a way that he has never done before. God has ceased to be a doctrine and has become a person. In some ways Job may know less about God than he did before. A number of his beliefs have been shattered. But he does have a deeper relationship with God than he did prior his suffering. He no longer takes the Deity for granted as a part of the good equals reward/bad equals punishment equation of the doctrine of retribution. And he knows that God has His eye on him and cares for him.

His new relational understanding causes him to recoil in humiliation from the dogmatic speeches he has made to his friends and the charges he has hurled at God. Bowing before the awesome whirlwind, he declares, "Therefore I despise myself, and repent in dust and ashes" (verse 6). The Hebrew verb here is not the usual one that Scripture employs for repentance of sins, but a word expressing grief and self-depreciation.

The patriarch's "repentance" has puzzled readers

and commentators. He has declared his innocence and upheld his integrity, and he was right in his claim that he had done nothing to deserve his suffering. What, then, does he have in mind here?

Commentators have made many suggestions as to why Job made his confession to God. But these in turn often raise other questions. For example, Daniel J. Simundson lists a number of possible reasons. [2]

1. That Job recognized the foolishness of his demand that God give him a visible sign of divine blessing and care. It is not wrong to want evidence of God's care and concern, but how much evidence should we expect, and when do we begin to rely on faith? Did Job show a lack of faith?

2. That he realized that God would never become the enemy of any of His children. "Perhaps Job needed to repent because he had come to think of God as a punisher, an avenger." [3]

3. That Job sensed that he had gone too far in his lament and complaint. We have a right to respond in grief to tragedy—God made us to react that way. But how far should our grief go? All of us know of people who have let some sad experience forever cripple their lives. When does grieving turn into distrust and rejection of God?

4. That Job came to acknowledge that he suffered from pride and lacked true humility. Simundson observes that it is often "the good people like Job who have the hardest time recognizing that they are sinful human beings." [4] Was it pride for Job to want to find intellectually satisfying solutions to every problem? Is it pride to expect God to answer our questions when we might not be able to understand if He did?

5. That the patriarch at last saw that he was depending on a secondhand religion based on the traditions and teachings of his community, not his own personal experience.

6. That Job sensed that he had been hostile to his friends. In his grief he had been rather insulting and wished on others the same kinds of suffering he was experiencing. But when does a cry of pain turn into sin?

In addition to those suggestions offered by Simundson, the repentance may be that Job has withdrawn his charges and grievances against God.

Edwin Good comments that Eliphaz had warped the whole discussion between Job and his friends into a false one of guilt and innocence. The men saw everything that happened in the world as either a punishment of someone's guilt or a reward for a person's purity. Job went along with their perspective until his encounter with God. Then he repented of such reasoning. [5] La Sor, Hubbard, and Bush see Job's repentance as an admission that he had complained against God because he had not known Him well enough. [6]

Whatever the reason—and Job may have had several—he repents of his previous attitude toward God, even though the Lord has regarded him all this time as upright and blameless. God now begins to publicly vindicate Job, as the patriarch had hoped for so long, but on His own terms. God must preserve His own freedom. He may do what we request, but it is always His own decision. Addressing Eliphaz, He declares, "My wrath is kindled against you and against your two friends; for you have not spoken of me what is right, as my servant Job has" (verse 7). God upholds Job as the one who has been right in the debate. The Deity is angry because they have acted as the Satan's agents in attempting to force Job to compromise his integrity.

Perhaps God singled out Eliphaz because he broke the silence and started the fruitless dialogue, because his speeches embodied many of the ideas that Bildad and Zophar only expanded, or because he was at first considerate of Job, then allowed his anger and frustration to overwhelm that initial respect. Or it could be still another example of the Old Testament literary pattern that only two people can address each other at a time. By being singled out by name, though, Eliphaz receives a greater rebuke than the others.

What does God mean when He says that Job spoke rightly of Him? Although the patriarch shared the doctrine of retribution with the other friends, he did recognize that reality was far more complex than his friends' theology allowed for. Eliphaz and the other friends held that suffering was the divine automatic punishment for guilt. Job raised doubts that life was that simple and easy and claimed that the innocent could suffer (as in his own case), while the guilty might escape punishment in this life.

But there might be still another factor, one that may disturb many devout believers. The key point of Job's self-defense has been that he believes that God is in some way involved with or behind his suffering. God may be acknowledging responsibility for what happened to Job in the presence of his friends, especially when we consider what the narrator has to say in verse 11.

The Lord tells the friends (verse 8) that they must offer sacrifices and ask Job to pray for them. (Verse 8 also repeats God's claim that Job has spoken truthfully about Him.) Like Abraham in Genesis 18, the patriarch will be their mediator to spare them from divine wrath. Job had earlier asked for a mediator—now he has become one himself. And in a most ironical twist of fate, the men who regarded Job as the object of divine wrath discover that they need him to spare them from that same wrath.

But perhaps God has still another reason for assigning Job such a task in addition to publicly vindicating him. God may be using it as a highly effective way of healing Job's grief.

It is a pattern in the Old Testament that after someone has complained about or protested against suffering, God then asks that individual to take responsibility for others. Jeremiah complained about God's dealing with him in Jeremiah 12. In response the Lord reminds him of his prophetic call and his duty to God's people. Naomi explodes in grief against God because of the death of her family, then begins to care for her widowed daughter-in-law Ruth.

Habakkuk protests God's apparent indifference to the suffering of His people, the Lord responds and speaks through the prophet, and the prophet finds himself praying in the manner of Job, "O Lord, I have heard of your renown, and I stand in awe, O Lord, of your work" (Hab. 3:2). Habakkuk must resume his duty of representing God before the people and in the process identify with God's feelings toward them.

One of the best ways of dealing with grief is to drown it in service to others. Job must now care for his

friends. Perhaps God gives us such responsibility because He wants us to feel, in our concern for others,
the love He has for all of us.

God may have also requested the sacrifices by the
friends and the prayer by Job as a way of reconciling
the men. The debate has almost destroyed their relationship, and God wants to restore their friendship.
Eliphaz, Bildad, and Zophar offer the requested sacrifices, and God accepts Job's prayer for them (Job 42:9),
foreshadowing James' famous statement about the
effectiveness of the prayer of a righteous person (James
5:16).

Once the men have been reconciled to each other,
God begins to restore Job's fortunes. Simundson observes that it may be significant that the restoration
begins only when the patriarch turns away from his
own problems and becomes active in the lives of
others. "There may well be something symbolic in
Job's ability now to focus attention on the needs of
others and not be preoccupied exclusively with his
own pain." [7]

God now gives Job twice as much material possessions as he had before (Job 42:10, 12), a fact that has
bothered many commentators and readers. Can anything recompense him for what he has gone through?
Other commentators have seen an interesting parallel
between the twofold restoration and the fact that
Israelite law required thieves to pay double when they
stole an ox, ass, or sheep. [8]

New children are born to Job, but he does not
receive twice as many as before. God gives him the
same number as his previous family—seven sons and
three daughters, a combination that, according to

ancient Canaanite stories, appears to be a particularly blessed one. Simundson suggests that the number of children was not doubled because it would be treating human lives as a commodity and increasing Job's pain. "Job does receive a new family. God blesses him with posterity. But the memory of what was lost will remain." [9] A new child can never replace a lost one.

The Lord also reverses the alienation that Job had complained of in Job 19:13-19. Family and friends come to eat with him (Job 42:11). God made human beings to live in community, and He now restores these vital relationships for the patriarch. The suffering man who felt so alone is now once more a part of his community.

Each person brings him a gold ring and a piece of money, a *qesitah*. It was not coinage as we know it—coinage was not used in the Mediterranean world until 700 B.C., and even later in Palestine—but a large unit of weight that also served as a unit of value. [10] William W. Hallo sees in the gift of the *qesitah* a reflection of the token prize awarded to the winner at the conclusion of a Sumerian disputation. [11] The gifts would have added up to a large sum and were clearly a mark of respect to an honored person rather than a gift to an impoverished one.

His family and friends "showed him sympathy and comforted him for all the evil that the Lord had brought upon him" (verse 11). [12] Here is undeniable acknowledgment that God assumed responsibility for permitting what had happened to Job. Although the Satan performed the direct attacks, God could have stopped him. But in His wisdom He chose not to.

The Satan has disappeared from the book. God

alone is sovereign, and He is willing to accept responsibility even for the bad things that happen under His
rule, as we see elsewhere in Scripture (cf. Ex. 4:11). Sin
seduces its victims into rejecting responsibility for
their actions (Gen. 3:12, 13), but righteous beings accept
the consequences for what they do. The Lord does not
tell Job about the role of the Satan. Perhaps He knows
that His servant is not ready to deal with it. Some
commentators have suggested that for Job to learn
about the Satan would have raised more questions and
made him even angrier at God.

All of us have had the experience of trying to
explain something, only to have the attempt misunderstood so that we wind up with more problems
than before. A study of political news stories and
headlines found that even the most careful denial of
an accusation can sometimes be interpreted as an
admission of the allegation. People hear everything
through the filter of their experiences and beliefs, and
this applies to spiritual things as well as everything
else. [13] For the time being God decided it was easiest to
accept blame until further revelation could open human insight to the complexity of the struggle between
good and evil.

Or it may be that God ignores the role of the Satan
because He wants the patriarch to first learn to trust
Him no matter what. Without such trust, any further
explanation would be bound to be misinterpreted. In
Job's case, such trust could have been more vital than
understanding the Satan's role in his suffering.

Many modern Christians with their greater knowledge of Satan have become so obsessed with him that
they have acted as if he were more powerful than God

Himself. It is far more important that we learn to have a relationship with God than that we know about the wiles of the devil. Nor must we jump to the conclusion that the Satan is directly behind all suffering. We, out of our fallen human natures, also inflict suffering on each other whether he instigates it or not, and some suffering just happens because we live in a creation in "bondage to decay" (Romans 8:21).

Job's new daughters receive special mention (Job 42:13-15). Part of that is an indication of his restored fortunes. Their beauty and the rich inheritances they have awaiting them will ensure good marriages for them and guarantee grandchildren so he will have a heritage and a kind of immortality through physical descendants. (Women normally did not inherit anything at their father's death.) [14] But the daughters also receive recognition in their own right. The patriarchal world of Job's time did not often pay attention to women, so to mention them here is a special honor.

Their names "represent natural feminine physical and spiritual charms enhanced by a perfumer's and beautician's art." [15] Jemimah means "dove"; Keziah means either "cassia" (or cinnamon), a substance used for perfume and incense, or perhaps "bow"; and Keren-happuch means "horn of antimony," a compound used by ancient women much as mascara is now. [16]

The restored Job lives a long and idyllic life and witnesses four generations of his new family. In words that described the goal of every ancient man, he died "old and full of days" (verse 17). [17] The Septuagint, wanting to make the ending of Job even more positive, adds a note to verse 17 that the patriarch will be raised in the resurrection from the dead.

But what have we learned from the book of Job? Is it just an ancient and pious story with little relevance to the tragedy and suffering that bombard us every day? Or does it still speak to us in our grief and pain? [18]

Job can teach us:

1. Suffering ultimately has no reason for being. There may be factors behind it, but no justifiable explanation. It is total irrationality, despite the attempts of some philosophers and religious groups to give it a place in God's scheme of things. Nor must we relegate it to some kind of divine educational tool. Though God can help us learn from it, He is not responsible for it. We may find ourselves tested by it, but God never intended that any of His creation should ever need such testing. Some have suggested that God uses it to remind us of our creature-liness. But it did not spring into existence for that reason.

2. While suffering can never be explained or justified, it can be redeemed. God suffers with us. [19] Job was God's suffering servant in the Satan's challenge in the heavenly assembly. But a greater Suffering Servant described by the prophet Isaiah came in the person of Jesus and shared our grief and pain with us—and went far beyond even the worst agony we may ever know. The cross is not just physical or emotional pain—it is spiritual anguish that no other being has or ever will suffer again. Job may have experienced the silence of a hidden God, but it was an insignificant pinprick compared to the sense of utter lostness at Calvary that drove Jesus to cry out, "My God, my God, why have you forsaken me?" (Matt. 27:46). Even God cannot really

explain suffering. He could only share it with us. Throughout eternity we will always be coming to the realization that His suffering was greater than all ours combined.

3. Ironic as it may seem, while God is not responsible for suffering, it can show both the power and love of God. John 9:1-38 tells of Jesus' healing of a man born blind. The disciples, steeped in the tradition that handicaps were punishment for sin, asked Jesus, "Rabbi, who sinned, this man or his parents, that he was born blind?" (verse 2). Jesus did not explain what had really caused the blindness. Instead, He answered, "Neither this man nor his parents sinned; he was born blind so that God's works might be revealed in him" (verse 3). As a result of the unfortunate man's suffering, God was given a chance to demonstrate His power.

Whatever the cause of suffering, God can use it to remind us that His love and power are greater than all evil and pain. Evil may be God's enemy, but it is never His rival. God may permit Satan to flaunt the inevitable consequences of evil, but He is always able to overcome it.

4. And finally, although God was not directly responsible for Job's suffering, He was willing to accept responsibility for the great freedom He has given His creation. The parent who sees the cruelty one of his children can do to another senses not only the pain of the injured child but another, far deeper hurt: that which comes from the fact that he or she brought these children into the existence that allows them to inflict such cruelty on each other.

But even more than that, God accepted responsibility for all suffering and for the guilt of those who caused it. Through His Son He took it with open arms and bore it until it killed His beloved Son. Job knew the grief of the loss of his children when that whirlwind swept their brother's house down upon them. No created being can ever know the pain the Father felt when Jesus hung on the cross.

The book of Job forcefully confronts us with the fact that there are mysteries that we will never be able to solve or understand. The book does not tie up all the loose ends. It shows us, not the cause of suffering, but how one person responded to it. Suffering will ever remain a mystery.

Experience tells us that evil will always ultimately self-destruct. The dramatic collapse of totalitarian governments during the last decade of the twentieth century demonstrates that evil consumes its own perpetrators and leads to chaos. But experience also reminds us that good only rarely triumphs in this life. In the present life new forms of evil will continue the mystery of suffering.

But more important than the question of suffering, the book of Job reminds us that beyond the whirlwind that destroys there is a God who loves and comforts. He does more than just speak to us—through Jesus Christ He has become one with us. Jesus' death is the most powerful vindication of Job possible. For those willing to listen and respond, Christ's death is the greatest argument that anyone can raise against the idea "that those who suffer are the worst sinners." [20] As God's servant Job once suffered, Jesus became the greater Suffering Servant.

He also drastically modified the concept of retribution when He said that God causes the sun to rise upon both the evil and the good, and the rain (a blessing in Palestine) to fall on both the just and the unjust (Matt. 5:45; cf. Job 38:25-27).

As I was making my final revisions to this book, my son, Tompaul, was with a group of other young people on a volunteer missionary project to a Caribbean island nation building an educational facility for a church. One day the group went to a beach resort for some relaxation. A rain storm suddenly blew up. Some of the young people retreated to their bus, but five of them took shelter under a tarp stretched between some palm trees. Lightning struck one of the trees, hurling the five youth several feet and knocking them unconscious. The adult leaders were able to revive four of them, but an 18-year-old boy died.

A girl with the group became angry at God for not protecting her new friend. Why had He not delivered him from "the fire of God" (Job 1:16)? Why had this happened to a young man involved in religious witness?

Such incidents cannot be explained. We can only cling to the knowledge that God—as He revealed to Job from the whirlwind and the rest of the world from the cross—is powerful enough to deal with any problem.

The Christian must always put the problem of suffering in the context of the One who has given us the greatest revelation of God so far. The New Testament demonstrates that God is big enough and loving enough to deal with the problem of evil and suffering because He met them head-on at Golgotha.

And that is the most important thing that we can

ever learn about suffering. With Him its whirlwinds
vanish, the sky clears, and a zephyr of love will caress
us for eternity.

---

[1] Craigie, *The Old Testament: Its Background, Growth, and Content*, p. 228.

[2] Simundson, *The Message of Job*, pp. 20-31.

[3] *Ibid.*, p. 27.

[4] *Ibid.*, p. 28.

[5] Good, "Job," in *Harper's Bible Commentary*, p. 431.

[6] La Sor, *Old Testament Survey*, p. 568.

[7] Simundson, p. 149.

[8] La Sor, p. 569, note 22.

[9] Simundson, p. 149.

[10] Jacob bought land at Shechem for 100 *qesitah* (Gen. 33:19). Since it appears only in Genesis and Joshua 24:32, the *qesitah* appears to be an ancient unit of value.

[11] William W. Hallo, "Sumerian Literature: Background to the Bible," *Bible Review*, June 1988, p. 33.

[12] The Hebrew of the text is the same as Job 2:11. Janzen suggests that the author may be implying a gentle irony between how the three friends and Job's family treated the patriarch (Janzen, *Job*, pp. 268, 269).

[13] Washington *Post*, Mar. 16, 1992, p. A3.

[14] Numbers 27 states that daughters inherit only if the father has no male heirs.

[15] Pope, *Job*, p. 353.

[16] Interestingly, ancient stories about the god Baal name his three daughters but not his seven sons.

[17] Cf. Gen. 25:8; 35:29; 50:23; 1 Chron. 29:28; Ps. 128:6; and Prov. 17:6.

[18] David Penchansky even goes as far as to say that "*there are in fact no answers in Job*" to the problem of the existence of disinterested piety and undeserved suffering (Penchansky, *The Betrayal of Gods*, p. 71). We would disagree with him, but the answers are more suggestive than definitive. Instead of giving neat explanations, God through inspiration wants us to keep struggling and thinking, and realize that all answers are incomplete and partial. That ultimately suffering is unexplainable.

[19] Even in the Old Testament God suffers with His people. For a helpful overview of this vital topic, see Terence E. Fretheim, *The Suffering of God: An Old Testament Perspective* (Philadelphia: Fortress Press, 1984).

[20] Fred B. Craddock, *Luke* (Louisville: John Knox, 1990), p. 168.

Selected Bibliography

Andersen, Francis I. *Job: An Introduction and Commentary*. Downers Grove, Ill.: Inter-Varsity Press, 1976.

Kelly, Balmer H. *The Book of Ezra; The Book of Nehemiah; The Book of Esther; The Book of Job (The Layman's Bible Commentary)*. Atlanta: John Knox Press, 1962.

Gibson, John C. L. *Job*. Philadelphia: Westminster Press, 1985.

Gladson, Jerry. *Who Said Life Is Fair? Job and the Problem of Evil*. Washington, D.C.: Review and Herald Pub. Assn. 1985.

Good, Edwin M. "Job." In *Harper's Bible Commentary*. Ed. James L. May, San Francisco: Harper and Row, 1988.

Janzen, J. Gerald. *Job*. Atlanta: John Knox Press, 1985.

Kidner, Derek. *The Wisdom of Proverbs, Job, and Ecclesiastes*. Downers Grove, Ill.: InterVarsity Press, 1985.

La Sor, William Sanford, David Allan Hubbard, and Frederic William Bush. *Old Testament Survey: The Message, Form, and Background of the Old Testament*. Grand Rapids: Eerdmans, 1982.

Murphy, Roland E. *Wisdom Literature and Psalms*. Nashville: Abingdon Press, 1983.

Pope, Marvin H. *Job*. Garden City, N. Y.: Doubleday and Co., 1965.

Selms, A. van. *Job: A Practical Commentary*. Grand Rapids: Eerdmans, 1985.

Simundson, Daniel J. *The Message of Job: A Theological Commentary*. Minneapolis: Augsburg, 1986.